Flamingo

Animal
Series editor: Jonathan Burt

Flamingo

Caitlin R. Kight

REAKTION BOOKS

To my family: my husband, Sasha; my parents, Fred and Stephanie; and my grandparents, Marvin, Norma, Fred and Barbara. You're the best flock a flamingo chick could wish for.

Published by
REAKTION BOOKS LTD
33 Great Sutton Street
London EC1V 0DX, UK
www.reaktionbooks.co.uk

First published 2015

Printed and bound in China by C&C Offset Printing Co. Ltd

A catalogue record for this book is available from the British Library

ISBN 978 1 78023 425 0

Contents

Introduction

Flamingos have been described as both the most charismatic of all bird species and one of the most recognizable.[1] While some might argue with the former claim, few would challenge the latter. Thanks to their bright, cheerful plumage, hefty, crooked bill and spindly legs – one often held aloft in that iconic balanced position – flamingos are instantly familiar to people around the world. This star power is probably also influenced by the fact that the birds occur naturally on five continents and in captivity on six. Because these birds are often referred to generically as 'pink flamingos', many people may not realize that there are actually six different species: American (also called Caribbean, Cuban or rosy, *Phoenicopterus ruber*); greater (*Phoenicopterus roseus*); Chilean (previously also known as red-kneed, *Phoenicopterus chilensis*); lesser (*Phoeniconaias minor*, though potentially soon to be renamed *Phoenicoparrus minor*); Andean (*Phoenicoparrus andinus*); and puna, or James's (*Phoenicoparrus jamesi*). Athough some researchers have argued that the American and greater flamingos are actually two subspecies of *Phoenicopterus ruber*, the most recent genetic analyses indicate that they are distinct species.

Not surprisingly, both common and scientific flamingo appellations nearly always refer to the birds' fiery plumage; references to flamingos' other unusual physical traits are also fairly common. In the ancient Mesopotamian empire of Akkadia, flamingos were

Lesser flamingos foraging at Lake Nakuru, Kenya.

called *issur nuri*, or 'bird of light'. Ancient Egyptians used a flamingo hieroglyph to write the word *dsr*, which could indicate not only the birds themselves, but also the colour red – or, more literally, 'flamingo-coloured'. Elsewhere in Africa, the Kikuyus (the largest tribe in Kenya), call flamingos *muhau*, a word that means 'long neck'. The ancient Arabic term *nuham* means 'flaming one', although both it and the medieval Arabic word *mirzam* derive from roots indicating a growling sound reminiscent of the birds' unmelodic vocalizations; *turundijan*, on the other hand, refers to flamingos' brilliant plumage.[2] Despite the prominence of Arabic in modern-day Egypt (it is the official state language), a Coptic influence resulted in locals' use of the word *basharush*, which translates to 'the thing which is red'.[3] Some authors have associated this with the Old French *bécaru*, used in the Provence area as a slang term for flamingos.[4] Another Arabic nickname is *rahu l-ma*, or 'aquatic crane'.

The Greeks referred to flamingos as φοινικόπτερος, meaning 'red-feathered' or 'red-winged'. The first half of the word derives from φοῖνιξ ('dark red'), which was also used to refer to the tanned Phoenician traders with whom the Greeks did business – hence the modern Greek word *phoinikopteros* and the Latinized version *phoenicopter*, the basis for the modern genus and family epithets for all six species. The Romans – with a little help from the Greeks – also gave us the other roots that appear in flamingos' scientific names. *Ruber* comes from the Latin for 'red', while *roseus* dates back to the Greeks (probably meaning, as it does in Latin, 'the pinkish-red colour of a rose'). The *-naias* in *Phoeniconaias* refers to the water-loving naiads of Greek myth, so lesser flamingos are 'dark red water-nymphs'. Perhaps the least sensible is *Phoenicoparrus*, which incorporates a form of the Latin word *parra*. Although some claim that this refers to a 'bird of ill omen', it may also simply mean

'unidentified bird' – thus an unidentified (or newly discovered) flamingo species.

Speakers of Romance languages can trace their words for flamingos back to the Latin *flamma*, meaning 'flame'; this eventually became *flamengo* in Portugal, *flamant* in France and *flamenco* in Spain. Once the Germanic *-ing* replaced the Latin suffixes, the English word *flamingo* was born. Some etymologists claim that this was only applied to birds after the fourteenth century, when Spanish-speakers first used *flamenca* to describe the Flemings, who were famous for having ruddy complexions (not unlike the ancient Phoenicians); if that is the case, then *flamengo* indicated 'a bird coloured like the Flemings'. One thing most scholars do

Greater flamingos in flight.

agree on is that there is no etymological connection between the word for the brightly coloured birds and the term referring to the vibrant Spanish style of dance.[5]

Flamingos' less poetic common names provide more straightforward information about each species: American, Chilean and Andean flamingos do, in fact, live in those regions; greater flamingos are the largest of the birds while lesser flamingos are the smallest; and the puna, or James's, flamingo was indeed discovered by a man named James (Henry Berkeley James), and inhabits high-altitude cold desert *puna* habitats in South America.

Flamingos have one of the best fossil records – described as 'unusually good' and 'particularly fine' – available for any bird species.[6] There have been sixteen fossil collections from six different geological epochs on five different continents. Flamingo-like fossils are known from the Eocene epoch (*c.* 50 million years ago), but some palaeontologists have also interpreted a few leg bone fragments as belonging to flamingo ancestors from the Late Cretaceous (100–66 million years ago). While flamingo bill morphology appears to have continued evolving even after the appearance of 'modern' flamingos 30 million years ago (in the Oligocene epoch), the birds' legs and feet had by then become the structures that we see today.

Despite the impressive age of the flamingo fossil record, recent genetic studies have suggested that Phoenicopteridae is actually one of the most recently evolved bird families. This group of birds likely emerged from its closest relatives approximately 4.37 million years ago; the common ancestor of the James's, Andean and lesser flamingos probably diverged around 2.6 million years ago, while the founder of the *Phoenicopterus* branch probably split off 2.3 million years ago.[7]

Despite the amount of information that palaeobiologists have managed to glean from the flamingo fossil record, scientists are still debating just where these birds are positioned in the avian family tree. Over the years, different researchers have used morphological, behavioural, developmental, genetic and/or medical observations to place flamingos with, variously, storks and herons, waterfowl and waders such as avocets and oyster-catchers.

Although there are a few remaining doubters, most taxono-mists agree that flamingos are most closely related to the grebes, together with whom they form a clade – a group of species and all their descendants, represented by a complete branch on the 'tree of life' – called Mirandornithes. This hypothesis is supported by multiple analyses of DNA, skeletal structure, egg morphology, nest remains and shared parasites; there is such a wealth of information that taxonomist Ernst Mayr claims that Mirandornithes is 'one of the best supported higher-level clades within modern birds'.[8] One question that remains, however, is whether the oldest ancestor of this group was aquatic like grebes and then moved to the shore like flamingos, or vice versa.

A grebe, from the bird family to which flamingos are probably most closely related.

Fossilized Phoenicopteridae nest that has flamingo-like eggs but grebe-like structure and composition; researchers think this belongs to an ancestor from which both groups of birds descended.

In his book *Flamingo City* (1950), George Kirby Yeates wrote that 'at close quarters the flamingo looks rather foolish' – not exactly high praise from someone who was otherwise quite a fan of the birds.[9] His assessment is not entirely inaccurate, however: all six species possess unwieldy bills and unusually long legs and necks – the latter of which can be held in quite awkward positions. Thanks to these shared traits, and of course the trademark pink coloration, it is easy to think, from a distance, that all flamingos look alike. However, variations in size, as well as degree and location of coloration, make it relatively easy to distinguish between adults of the different species.

The American flamingo stands 120–40 cm (4–4 ft 5 in.) tall and has a wingspan of approximately 150 cm (60 in.). Despite its impressive height, this species weighs only 2.2–2.8 kg (5–6 lb). As is the case with all flamingos, males are generally both taller and heavier than females. American flamingos are the most thoroughly colourful of the six species, with the brightest birds achieving a dark rosy or even orange hue across all of their feathers.

The most vivid coloration is found on the birds' heads, necks and breasts, although there are also bright patches on their flanks and under their tails. As is true for all six species of flamingo, the front portion of the wing is reddish, while the tips and back half are black. These contrasting hues are not often visible when the birds are stationary and have their wings folded back, but create an easily identifiable pattern during flight. The reddish-pink scapulars, or shoulder-blade feathers, usually hang down along the birds' sides and over their tails; however, as with all flamingos, these may be erected if the birds are alarmed or angry. The legs of this species are pink, with a vivid red 'knee' joint. (Flamingos, like other walking birds, are digitigrade, meaning that they walk on their toes. Thus, although the joint at the mid-point of flamingos' legs appears comparable to the human knee, it is actually akin to our ankle; their true knees are located much further up and closer to their bodies). The bill of the American flamingo is four-toned: black at the tip, orange in the middle, yellow at the top of the base and red at the bottom of the base. The eyes are light yellow.[10]

As you might predict for two birds that were formerly thought to be the same species, American and greater flamingos share many of the same physical traits. Like its New World cousin, the greater flamingo is quite tall – in fact, at 110–50 cm (45–60 in.) and with a record height of 187 cm (73 in.), it is the tallest of all six species. It has an impressive wingspan of 140–70 cm (55–65 in.) and weighs 2–4 kg (4 lb 6 oz–8 lb 13 oz). Also like the American, the greater flamingo has a black-tipped bill, though this tip is smaller and gives way to pink coloration that extends up to the bird's pale yellow eyes. The legs of the greater flamingo are more uniformly pink, though some younger birds display darker patches around the joints. Although this species has noticeable scapulars, one striking difference is their colour: these feathers,

as well as those covering the chest, neck and head, are usually pale pink or even white; the greater flamingo is the least pink of all six species, and even the most colourful birds rarely approach the hue of their close American cousins. In most greater flamingos, the pinkest feathers are the wing coverts, or those covering the flight feathers. Although these can be a deep crimson, their position underneath the drooping scapulars may make the colour hard to see until the birds take flight.[11]

American flamingo.

The third member of the genus *Phoenicopterus*, the Chilean flamingo, is probably the species described by Charles Darwin in his *A Naturalist's Voyage Round the World* (1860).[12] These birds so closely resemble the other two members of their genus that, along with the greater flamingo, they were once considered to

Greater flamingo.

Chilean flamingo standing on its nest at the Wildfowl & Wetlands Trust (WWT), Slimbridge, Gloucestershire.

be a subspecies of *P. ruber*. Chileans achieve heights of 110–30 cm (45–50 in.) and are shorter than greater flamingos mainly because their legs are not as long as those of the latter. Chilean flamingos have a wingspan of 120–50 cm (45–60 in.) and weigh 2.5–3.5 kg (5 lb 8 oz–7 lb 11 oz). Although considerably paler than the American flamingo, they are still more colourful than the greater: their feathers are mostly pale pink, though whiter on the head and with crimson in the scapulars and forewings. During the breeding season, there are also brighter rosy areas on the birds' throats and chests. Like their eyes, the legs of the Chilean flamingo are yellow, or sometimes yellowish grey – markedly lighter than those of the other *Phoenicopterus* birds. As in the other species the joints and feet are bright pink, only in these birds the contrast with the rest of the leg is much more obvious. Again the bill is black-tipped, transitioning into a white or pale pink base. Variations in bill patterns can be used to reliably identify individual birds.[13]

The Andean flamingo is both the largest of the three South American species and the one that displays the greatest amount of black coloration. It is 100–140 cm (40–55 in.) tall and has a wingspan of 100–160 cm (40–60 in.). Andean flamingos weigh up to 4 kg (8 lb 13 oz), which, given their relative shortness, makes these fairly sturdy birds. From a distance, Andeans can appear to be one solid colour, but in reality their plumage is somewhat speckled. The head, neck and chest are deep pink (sometimes described as purplish or wine-red), while their lower breasts and backs are spotted with darker pink against a lighter pink background. The 'pink-red' of the wings is only obvious when the wings are outstretched, but the black outer feathers are visible even with the wings folded back; they appear as black triangles on the birds' rumps. The black-tipped bill is pale yellow at the base and is marked by a red spot between the nostrils. As with the Chilean flamingo, subtle differences between birds can be used to identify particular individuals. The legs and feet of this species are yellow, but the eyes are orange-brown.[14]

The smallest South American flamingo is the puna, standing just 102–10 cm tall (40–43 in.), with a wingspan of approximately 100 cm (40 in.) and an average weight of only 2 kg (4 lb 6 oz). The punas' plumage is predominantly whitish, with a pink wash on the head and upper neck, rosy scapulars and a rosy speckling across the chest that only appears during the breeding season. These birds also have red and black wings, but the black is less noticeable than in the Andean when the wings are folded. Puna flamingos have the most intricately coloured bill of all flamingos:

the short black tip gives way to an orange-yellow base that is bordered near the face by a narrow red band extending back to the birds' dark brown eyes. Their legs and feet are orange-red.[15] A defining feature of both *Phoenicoparrus* species – but one that would only be noticeable at close proximity – is their lack of a hind toe, or hallux. Thus while all other flamingos have four toes, the Andean and puna only have three.

In regions inhabited by both greater and lesser flamingos, it is usually fairly easy to tell the two species apart. Unlike their much taller companions, lesser flamingos stand at a maximum height of 100 cm (40 in.) – the same size as their wingspan – and weigh only about 2 kg (4 lb 6 oz). In fact, these birds are so small that their heads only reach chest height on greater flamingos. Although not as dark as their New World cousins, lesser flamingos are usually more obviously pink than greater flamingos; this is especially true of the head and neck. There is dark pink mottling on the back and wings, but this species still shows the pink/ black wing pattern characteristic of all flamingos in flight. Lesser flamingos are the only species with an all-dark bill: it looks black from a distance, but in fact has a dark red base transitioning into a black tip. The birds also have a dark red eye mask and bright yellow eyes – a combination that makes them look fierce, even demonic. Their legs are pink, and they possess a hallux that is reduced, or relatively small compared to that observed in the *Phoenicopterus* species. This makes their overall

Puna flamingo at WWT Slimbridge.

Lesser flamingos
in the wild.

foot morphology intermediate to that observed in the other two genera of flamingos – adding support to the recent suggestion that lesser flamingos should be reclassified from *Phoeniconaias* to *Phoenicoparrus*.[16]

Perhaps the most distinguishing feature of any flamingo is its colour. This trait is caused by the presence of carotenoids, pigments made up of carbon and hydrogen with a little oxygen sometimes thrown in for good measure. Carotenoids are produced by photosynthetic organisms such as plants, algae and some bacteria and fungi. Animals that eat these organisms inherit their carotenoids, sometimes altering them slightly during the metabolic process and sometimes keeping them in their original condition; either way, the pigments are eventually stored in the animals' own tissues, where they are responsible for creating shades of yellow, orange, red and, of course, pink.[17]

Although it is often said that flamingos are pink because they eat shrimp, this is only true of individuals of the larger species, which may feed on small aquatic crustaceans known as brine shrimp (*Artemia* spp.). The more common sources of carotenoids are cyanobacteria, algae and phytoplankton such as diatoms. These provide flamingos with five major pigments: echinenone, phoenicoxanthin, astaxanthin, phoenicopterone and, most importantly, canthaxanthin; fucoxanthin has also been isolated from Andean and puna flamingos. Cumulatively, these provide colour for things as diverse as skin, blood, the yolks of eggs and the birds' bright feathers. Flamingo coloration is so intense not only because of the large amount of carotenoids they consume – these pigments are thought to account for as much as 0.1 per cent of the dry weight of each bird's annual diet – but also because of the efficiency with which they are metabolized. Possession of this skill is noticeable in American flamingos, which have the brightest plumage of all six species and also the highest proportion of pink across the entire body. Different hues result from variations in the identity and quantity of prey items in each bird's diet. Juveniles are not pink at all, despite receiving carotenoids from their parents; depending on the species, young birds will

Chemical structure of canthaxanthin, one of the most important carotenoids responsible for flamingo coloration.

not begin to shift from their original greyish-white coloration to their brighter adult plumage until they are anywhere from two to four years old.

Flamingo feathers rapidly lose their colouration once shed, and scientists have long pondered how the birds could manage to stay so pink between moults. In greater flamingos, at least, it turns out that preen oil contains the carotenoid canthaxanthin, which allows the fluid to be used as a sort of cosmetic.[18] The birds first rub their cheeks directly on their preen glands, which are located under their tails; they then use their faces as paintbrushes, transferring the oil to their necks, breasts and back feathers. Although preening behaviour is generally positively related to intensity of coloration, the preen oil pigmentation varies seasonally, such that the highest carotenoid concentration overlaps with the breeding display period just before the nesting season. This suggests that flamingos use the pink coloration to attract mates; it serves not just as a pretty hue but as an indication that the animals are able to locate food resources and metabolize them efficiently. Potential partners appear to find this signal very sexy: researchers have found that the most colourful flamingos pair up and begin breeding earlier than their less colourful counterparts.

Another remarkable feature of flamingos is their bill morphology. The bills of all six species have a characteristic bend in the middle. This helps keep the width of the gap between the top and bottom portions of the bill consistent along its entire length, thus improving feeding efficiency. The bend has been said to give the birds a 'haughty appearance' and has earned the greater flamingo an Arabic nickname meaning 'camel of the sea'.[19]

The ubiquity of the 'crooked' bill across all flamingo species belies the differences that can be observed between the two distinct beaks found among the Phoenicopteridae: shallow-keeled,

possessed by the larger species (American, Chilean and greater), and deep-keeled, possessed by the smaller species (Andean, puna and lesser). The names reflect differences in the shapes of the upper mandibles. In shallow-keeled birds, the upper half of the bill is the same width, or sometimes a bit wider, than the lower. As a result, the former 'fits over the latter like the lid of

Close-up view of
deep-keeled
Andean (top) and
puna (bottom)
flamingo bills.

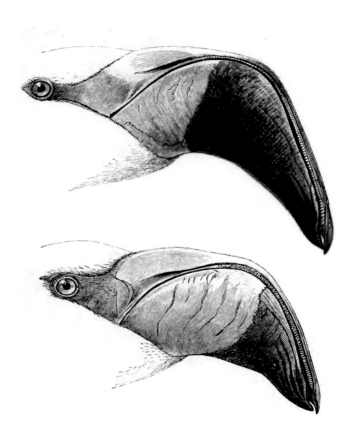

a box, leaving the gape at the sides of the bill'.[20] In deep-keeled
birds, however, this relationship is reversed: the upper bill is
much narrower than the lower and therefore nestles snugly
within it, and the gape can only be seen when looking down
from above.

Despite these differences, both types of bill do share one thing
in common: they are quite large relative to the birds' slender

heads and necks. Flamingos are able to support these weighty-looking structures because the bills are very porous, which not only makes them easier to heft in terrestrial settings but also allows them to float across the surface of the water while the birds feed. In all flamingos the lower bill narrows to a sharp tip that appears to function as a sort of funnel when the adults pass food from their mouths into those of their chicks.

The shallow-keeled bill of the American flamingo, in both open and closed positions.

25

Close-up of the narrow upper mandible of a puna, or James's, flamingo.

Another common feature of all flamingo bills is lamellae, small projections found along the inner surfaces and, in all but the American and greater flamingos, the edges of the bill. The exact size, shape, number and orientation of lamellae vary throughout the bill and from one species to the next, but all are united in a single purpose: to filter flamingos' tiny prey out of the water. In shallow-keeled bills, the lamellae are coarser and more widely spread, which is why American, Chilean and greater flamingos eat larger prey items; the dense positioning of lamellae in Andean, puna and lesser flamingos allows them to target much smaller food. Collected prey items are directed towards the back of the throat by spines on the birds' palates and tongues. The latter are associated with a vascular structure called the paralingual sinus, which comprises erectile tissue in the tongue and floor of the mouth. This feature, unique among birds but common across all six flamingo species, provides a sturdiness that probably improves feeding efficiency.[21]

Other remarkable characteristics of flamingo bills were famously described by the evolutionary biologist Stephen Jay Gould in his classic essay 'The Flamingo's Smile'. Gould's observations rely heavily on those of several much earlier naturalists, including the Greek satirist Menippus (third century BCE), French medical professor Guillaume Rondelet (Rondeletius, sixteenth century), Danish physician Ole Worm (Olaus Wormius, early seventeenth century) and British natural historian Nehemiah Grew (late seventeenth century).[22] What these men all noticed was that flamingos hold their lower bills fairly rigid while moving their upper bills; this is in direct contrast with most other jawed

Maxillary lamellae in a flamingo bill.

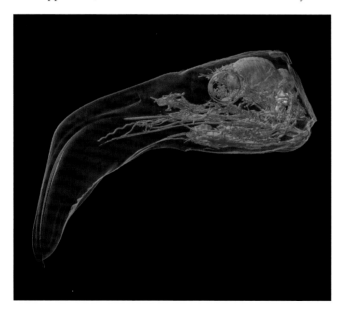

Erectile tissue in the bottom of a flamingo's mouth (indicated by the dense vascularization shown in red).

animals, including humans, in which the upper half of the jaw is held stationary while the lower half can move up and down and, to some extent, from side to side. Flamingos are able to achieve this 'reverse' movement thanks to a ball-and-socket joint between the two halves of the bill, allowing motion in either direction. The size difference between the upper and lower mandibles also represents a reversal from the norm. Whereas it is generally more common for the upper jaw to be bigger than the lower, the opposite is true for flamingos, as discussed above. Overall, these variations allow the anatomical tops of flamingo bills to be their functional bottoms, and vice versa – a trait observed very infrequently throughout the animal kingdom.

All flamingos have webbed feet, which not only give the birds stability when walking on mud, but also improve their efficiency while swimming. Another shared characteristic is possession of 23 elongated vertebrae – only two more than are found in geese. Observers who approach flamingos closely enough may be able to see kinks in the birds' necks where each vertebra is positioned. This view may also allow a glimpse of the saline solution that flamingos excrete from their nostrils in an effort to rid themselves of excess salt. This is produced by the birds' 'salt glands', a pair of structures located internally, just above the eye sockets.

Sight has only been studied in lesser flamingos, but it is not unreasonable to assume that vision in the other five species is similar to that of their diminutive relatives. Researchers found that the birds have a narrow but long frontal visual field, the lower boundary of which appears to be marked by their own bill tips. This arrangement seems out of place in filter-feeding flamingos, as it is generally more common in birds that perform directed pecking movements with their beaks. One explanation for this characteristic is that it may help parent flamingos improve their aim when delivering food into the mouths of their young. Lesser flamingos have also been found to possess large blind spots above and behind their heads. Given that these birds spend a large portion of their time standing with their heads positioned upside-down, this means that they cannot see into the water at their feet, or in the direction towards which they are walking; scientists hypothesize that flamingos' characteristic head-sweeping movements may allow them to periodically scan these blind spots in order to avoid being surprised by a predator.[23] Although some have claimed that flamingos' eyes are larger than their brains, there appear to be no scientific sources backing up this assertion, and no individual flamingo researchers seem willing to go on record to confirm it.

Despite the fact that flamingo fossils have been unearthed in Australia and Antarctica, the birds have not inhabited those continents for thousands, or even millions, of years. Researchers theorize that flamingos in these areas were driven to extinction by habitat loss associated with climate change. Today free-living flamingos can be found in North America (American), South America (Andean, Chilean and puna), Europe (greater), Africa (lesser and greater) and Asia (lesser and greater).

Although it was long thought that flamingos originated in the Old World and then colonized the New, the most recent genetic evidence suggests otherwise. Shallow-keeled flamingos almost certainly evolved in the Americas, and the same is likely also true of the deep-keeled species. However, researchers would like to analyse DNA samples from ancient Australian specimens to flesh out their understanding of the phoenicopter family tree. Given current data, the most likely scenario is that flamingos emerged in the western hemisphere and then spread eastward to colonize the Old World.

Flamingos of all species, and on all continents, are found in habitats linked by a single common feature: shallow saline pools.

Aerial view of Lake Nakuru, Kenya, a typical flamingo habitat.

These can be fed by underwater springs, ocean waves, rivers and, perhaps most importantly, rain. Water in flamingo habitats has been measured at over twice the salinity of the ocean and may contain sulphates and other compounds that can be distasteful or even harmful in large doses. Although this is hardly a welcoming environment to humans, it is quite pleasant for organisms such as brine shrimp, small molluscs, diatoms and cyanobacteria – all potential prey items for flamingos. Because so few animals can tolerate extremely salty environments or figure out how to collect the tiny particles of food available there, flamingos have been able to exploit this niche virtually uncontested.

In order to take advantage of habitats with proper water depth and the most flamingo-friendly pH, the birds must be willing to fly far and wide, often at a moment's notice. Migration among sites is seen throughout the year but is particularly common during the breeding season, when dietary needs are highest. Regular commutes of 100–200 km (60–125 mi.) between breeding and feeding grounds are not uncommon, and maximum flight distances may approach 1,500 km (930 mi.) in a single trip; one greater flamingo was even observed to make a migration flight that lasted fifteen hours straight. Birds cover ground between suitable habitats by flying at speeds of 50–70 km/h (30–45 mph), with a maximum recorded flight velocity of 76 km/h (47 mph).[24] Groups of flamingos increase their migration efficiency by flying in a V-formation.

One of the greatest remaining mysteries of flamingos is how the birds know where to go when they relocate. The existence of particular destinations can be learned from experience, as

Range of the Andean flamingo.

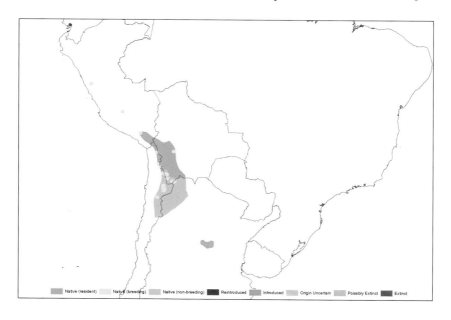

Native (resident) Native (breeding) Native (non-breeding) Reintroduced Introduced Origin Uncertain Possibly Extinct Extinct

| Native (resident) | Native (breeding) | Native (non-breeding) | Reintroduced | Introduced | Origin Uncertain | Possibly Extinct | Extinct |

Range of the
Chilean flamingo.

in geese; however, it is unclear what cues flamingos use to predict whether distant haunts are dry or have recently seen rain.
Another unanswered question is why the birds decide to leave
habitats when they do. On several occasions researchers have
seen flamingos depart wetlands where remaining food levels
are more than adequate. Thus the birds' movements appear
to be driven by something other than just dietary need. They
are perhaps more accurately described as 'nomadic' than
'migratory'.

Andean, Chilean and puna flamingos find their saltwater
habitat in the form of lakes on high-altitude plateaus in the
Andes. All three varieties are found in Peru, Chile, Bolivia and
Argentina; Chileans also sometimes appear in Paraguay, Uruguay
and Brazil. Although they often intermingle, the species have

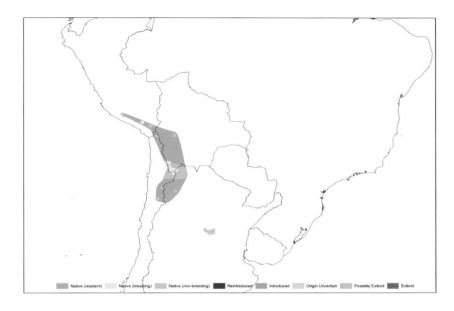

different altitude preferences. Chilean flamingos can be found from sea level up to 4,500 m (14,800 ft); Andean flamingos are mostly found above 2,500 m (8,200 ft); and puna flamingos, which have the most restricted range, are found predominantly in locations above 3,500 m (11,500 ft).

The remoteness of these mountainous habitats and the birds' frequent and unexpected movements between lakes make it extremely hard to census South American flamingos. However, current population estimates stand at approximately 34,000 Andean, 200,000 Chilean and 100,000 puna flamingos. The last figure is particularly impressive considering that the puna flamingo was thought to be extinct until it was rediscovered in 1956. Unfortunately, its conservation status is still in question and, along with the Chilean flamingo, it is currently listed as

Range of the puna flamingo.

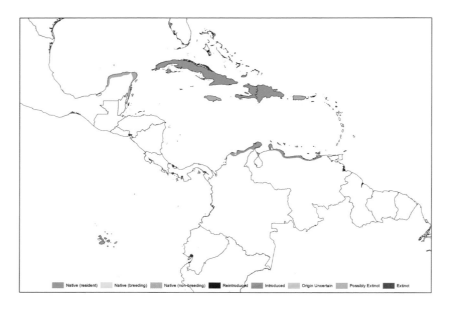

Native (resident)   Native (breeding)   Native (non-breeding)   Reintroduced   Introduced   Origin Uncertain   Possibly Extinct   Extinct

Range of the American flamingo.

'near threatened'; Andean flamingos are considered 'vulnerable'. Worries over these species stem not so much from current numbers of breeding birds, but from the fact that long-term population stability is threatened by anthropogenic disturbance and habitat destruction.

The final New World flamingo, the American, is the only one of the six species that does not share a part of its range with a fellow flamingo. It dwells in lagoons and other brackish coastal waters throughout the Caribbean, from the northern tip of the Yucatán Peninsula eastward to the Bahamas, Cuba, Hispaniola, Turks and Caicos, and southern Florida, as well as southward to the north coast of South America, in Colombia, Venezuela and Suriname. All told, there are approximately 260,000 to 330,000 adult flamingos across the Caribbean region, plus a small

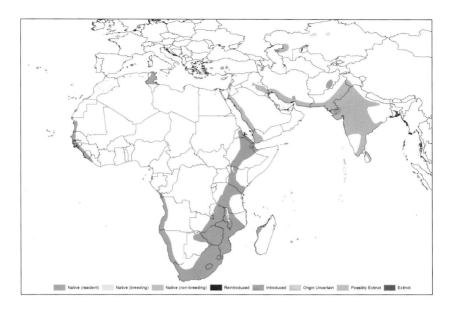

Native (resident)   Native (breeding)   Native (non-breeding)   Reintroduced   Introduced   Origin Uncertain   Possibly Extinct   Extinct

population of about 500 birds living on the Galapagos Islands. Because of its large range and healthy numbers, the American flamingo is of 'least conservation concern'.

The two Old World species, greater and lesser flamingos, often co-occur. For instance, both are found along Africa's west coast, along its southern tip and on Madagascar, and in the Great Rift Valley. In the Valley, they visit saline and soda lakes such as Elmenteita, Bogoria, Magadi, Sonnachi and Nakuru; however, Lake Natron (Tanzania) is generally considered the most important of these given that it is the breeding ground used by as much as 90 per cent of the entire lesser flamingo population, as well as by some of their larger relatives.

Both types of flamingo can also be found in the Rann of Kutch, a seasonal salt marsh spanning northeastern India and

Range of the greater flamingo.

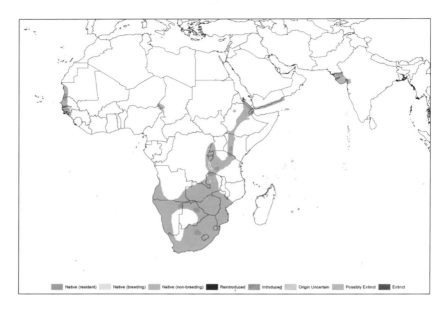

Native (resident)   Native (breeding)   Native (non-breeding)   Reintroduced   Introduced   Origin Uncertain   Possibly Extinct   Extinct

Range of the lesser
flamingo.

southeastern Pakistan. Lesser flamingos are not found elsewhere, but greaters may turn up anywhere in India and Sri Lanka, as far north as Iran and Kazakhstan and throughout the Mediterranean. France's Camargue region hosts the world's most northerly breeding colony of greater flamingos. The Camargue is western Europe's largest river delta; there, flamingos utilize brine lagoons and saline *étangs*, or lakes. The only other such colony in Europe is in Fuente de Piedra, Spain.

Although greater flamingos are the most widespread of all the Phoenicopteridae, they are not the most numerous; their worldwide population has been estimated at 550,000 to 680,000 adults, which pales in comparison to the 2.2 to 3.2 million estimated for lesser flamingos. Surprisingly, though, the former species is classified as being of least conservation concern, while the latter is considered near threatened. Lesser flamingos find themselves in this precarious position because of threats to their habitat in general, and Lake Natron in particular.[25] While the degradation of a single lake may not seem too serious given how many alternatives are available across the African continent, lesser flamingos are incredibly loyal to their former breeding sites, and therefore may be unwilling (or unable) to move elsewhere.

1 Flamingo Behaviour

Although the Phoenicopteridae are an understudied group relative to many other avian families, they are by no means strangers to ornithologists. Flamingos were observed and described as long ago as the fourth century BCE, and the first anatomical analysis of the birds appears to have been conducted in the early second century CE.[1] In his groundbreaking series *Histoire naturelle des oiseaux* (*Natural History of Birds*, published between 1749 and 1804), Georges-Louis Leclerc, Comte de Buffon, reviewed all that was then known about phoenicopters. Thanks to his liberal quoting from a variety of early texts, we have records of historical flamingo lore from sources that have now been lost.[2]

Prior to the 1950s, only a handful of flamingo studies had been performed in the West. The birds received more attention in the East thanks to the work of the great Indian ornithologist Salim Ali (1896–1987). Advances in transportation and field equipment have facilitated a global boom in flamingo literature over the past several decades. Scientists have recently begun to capitalize on the long-term datasets being generated at permanent flamingo field sites such as Tour du Valat, a research station established in 1954 by Luc Hoffmann in the saline wetlands of southern France.[3] A good deal has also been learned from studies on captive flamingos, such as those breeding at the

Slimbridge Wildfowl & Wetlands Trust in Gloucestershire in the UK and the Philadelphia Zoo in the U.S.

After their stunning colour, perhaps the next most iconic thing about flamingos is their tendency to stand on one leg. A modern joke suggests that flamingos adopt this position because they would fall over if they lifted up both limbs.[4] Not content with this pragmatic explanation, scientists have long searched for the biological underpinnings of the unusual posture. One suggestion was that it permitted the birds to limit muscle fatigue to one leg, allowing them to respond more easily to emergencies such as sudden attacks from predators. Another idea was that the stance facilitated heat retention, in much the same way that folding arms across the chest maintains warmth in humans. Scientists debated the merit of these two main theories for years, but studies conducted in 2010 and 2011 provided increasing evidence for the latter. Specifically, researchers have shown that flamingos stand on one leg more often in cooler temperatures. Furthermore, unipedally resting birds take longer to initiate forward movement, suggesting that there is no muscular benefit to resting on one leg.[5] Although the birds seem to handle this tricky position with the grace and confidence of ballerinas, it is probably not very stable: the length of one-legged resting periods has been shown to decrease on windier days, indicating that, even for flamingos, it is not easy to maintain balance while 'flamingoing'.

Investigations of stance laterality, or the propensity to stand on one leg rather than the other, suggest a potential correlation between which leg is held aloft and which side of the body the head is rested on. Since there seem to be both individual-level and flock-level preferences towards bending the neck to the right, this suggests that, like humans, flamingos have a right-side bias.[6] A study of captive birds found that 'left-handed' flamingos are more likely to become involved in aggressive encounters. This, along with the fact that birds in the same position can more easily stand side by side without bumping into each other, indicates that laterality may promote flock cohesion.

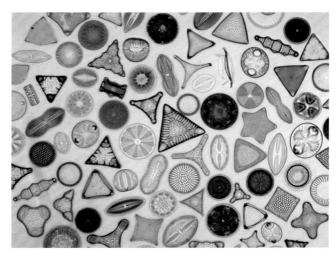

Diatoms, a popular flamingo prey item, as visualized by a compound microscope at 125× magnification.

Flamingo fare includes a variety of microorganisms, ranging from cyanobacteria, algae and diatoms to larger copepods, fly larvae and plant seeds. The three largest flamingo species are generalists, capable of taking advantage of a range of available prey, while the three smallest species are specialists dependent on 'blooms', or population explosions, of single-celled organisms; lesser flamingos are particularly fond of the algae Spirulina, while Andean and puna flamingos frequently target diatoms. Adults and juveniles of multiple species have been observed eating mud, and stomachs of several autopsied birds have been found to contain *only* mud. This suggests that flamingos are able to extract nutrients from prey items buried deep within the substrate, and/or potentially even from the substrate itself. However, it is likely that this option is reserved for only those times when other food sources are scarce. When flamingos do resort to eating mud, their feeding activities leave 'ronds', described by the ornithologist Étienne Gallet as 'basin-like depressions' that 'look like deserted tables'.[7]

Food preferences are driven by variations in bill morphology: while the diminutive lesser flamingo can filter out particles as small as 0.01 × 0.05 mm (0.0004 × 0.002 in.), its largest cousins, the American and greater flamingos, eat items up to 6 mm (0.24 in.) in length. However, all species can adjust their gapes in order to alter the 'porosity' of their filters to suit whatever prey are available;[8] they appear to use both taste and touch to sense when these adjustments are necessary. Food items are directed into the mouth by means of a 'lingual back-and-forth pump'.[9] Flamingos only move their tongues laterally (out and back), rather than from side to side. By doing this rapidly – as fast as twenty outward pumps per second in the lesser flamingo – the birds can flush an impressive volume of water past their lamellae each day. The ability to process this much fluid is essential given the density of prey items in the water column. Lesser flamingos, for instance, need to consume approximately 60 grams (2 oz, dry weight) of food each day, and prey items are found at an average density of 3 grams per litre (0.03 oz per gal.). This means that each bird needs to filter an astounding 20 litres (5 gal.) of water daily.

Flamingos can successfully feed even when prey densities drop as low as 1 gram per litre (0.009 oz per gal.). However, because they burn more energy than they gain once densities dip below 3 grams per litre (0.03 oz per gal.), these conditions will prompt the birds to relocate to another food patch. The need to find adequately stocked feeding sites causes flamingos to range quite widely: greaters, for instance, are known to forage up to 100 km (60 mi.) away from breeding colonies. Birds may head to alternative wetlands on their own, or may congregate in 'departure groups' that leave the breeding colony each day at dusk.[10] Flamingos limit the bulk of their feeding activities to the early morning, late afternoon and even the middle of the night. Nighttime feeding is a useful way of consuming extra calories that could not be located during the day, and may also be a handy method of avoiding the intense midday heat.[11] This feeding technique gives the birds plenty of time to rest during the middle portion of the day, during which they may spend as much as 30 per cent of their time preening to cleanse their feathers of salt collected while foraging in alkaline waters.

Flamingos can feed while either walking through shallower water or swimming through deeper water; they frequently submerge either part or all of their heads under the water's surface in order to access prey items. However, this is a simplistic description of the feeding process, and belies the existence of species-specific adaptations used to maximize access to the choicest foods. Lesser flamingos, for instance, sweep their bills

An American
flamingo foraging.

42

back and forth at a depth of about 3 cm (1 in.). Puna and Chilean flamingos repeatedly place their bills down and pick them back up, concentrating on specific spots in the water. American, Chilean and greater flamingos sometimes kick or stomp their feet to stir potential prey up into the water column. 'Treading', a more exaggerated version of this tactic, is used by the three largest species: it involves turning in a full circle while rapidly paddling the feet. Although more common in American, Chilean and greater flamingos, upending may also be used by all species to reach distant prey in deeper water. However, while flamingos are quite capable of swimming, they have not been observed to feed and swim simultaneously. When feeding in shallow areas, flamingos eat while walking forward (never backwards), trailing their bills along the surface of the mud. Because the birds adjust their feeding techniques depending on which prey items are present at any given time, it has been hypothesized that flamingos may keep an eye on the feeding behaviours of their flock-mates in order to determine the quality of particular food patches.[12]

Although use of these sorts of social cues often leads to competition and aggression in other species, this is not generally an issue for flamingos. In the Old World lesser and greater flamingos can share space peacefully because they have minimal overlap in prey species; additionally greater flamingos prefer less alkaline waters and stick closer to the shore. Similar spatial separations have been observed in the New World among Chilean, Andean and puna flamingos. Because flamingo prey are often found in incredibly high densities, thousands of flamingos can forage within a single wetland without competing for each other's food. Furthermore, depleted food stocks can regenerate within just a couple of weeks, permitting the birds to revisit favourite hunting grounds fairly frequently.

The formation of large feeding flocks may actually be beneficial, as it allows flamingos to use their own bodies to create calm patches buffered from the wind. There is also safety in numbers: many flamingo observers over the centuries have noted that there is usually at least one bird on alert at all times, ready to use its trumpet-like voice to alert its foraging neighbours to the presence of danger. Surprisingly, the main source of tension at feeding sites is encounters between younger and older birds. Adult flamingos appear to have little patience for juveniles and expect the latter to give way; when they do not, these encounters may result in aggression. The one time that this expectation may be relaxed is during external disturbance events (such as visitations by humans), since wary flamingos tend to draw closer together while feeding.[13]

As in many other species, feeding must also be accompanied by drinking, and that is something of a tricky proposition for birds in such salty habitats. Although the birds are capable of filter-feeding even in the most alkaline of waters, doing so appears to necessitate frequent breaks and repeated bill-cleansing.[14] Where no fresh water is available, flamingos have been known to drink ocean-strength saltwater. However, they appear to prefer fresh water, and quickly aggregate to take advantage of temporary pools of collected rainwater. The animals are sparing in their use of water, drinking for only a few seconds before ceding their position to the next thirsty bird in the queue. Flamingo expert Leslie Brown reports that he watched the birds comfortably drinking spring water so hot they could not stand in it without hopping from foot to foot; upon dunking a thermometer into the hot spring, Brown discovered that it was 68°c (154°F), or the approximate temperature of a hot cup of coffee.[15]

Like many other species of bird, flamingos communicate using both acoustic and visual signals. Surprisingly, their vocalizations

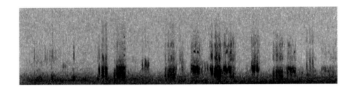

Sonogram of a 12-second recording of a Chilean flamingo vocalization; time is shown on the horizontal axis, and frequency (ranging from approximately 1–9 kHz) is shown on the vertical axis.

have received little scientific attention despite the fact that all species are highly gregarious, aggregating in colonies so noisy that some visitors have said that the sounds of the birds were more memorable than their striking plumage or behaviour. Flamingos produce many different vocalizations, ranging from rasps and grunts to honks and screeches; because of this variety, it is not easy to summarize each species' voice. American and greater flamingos have a goose-like sound.[16] Chilean flamingos, with their slightly higher-pitched voices, sound more like ducks. Andean flamingos have moderately nasal, high-pitched voices and sound rather like doves that have been pinched mid-coo. The voices of puna flamingos, on the other hand, have a squeaky quality reminiscent of the sound of a squeegee dragged across wet glass; they also whistle. This is also somewhat true for lesser flamingos, which, as might be expected given their size, have the highest-pitched voices of all six species. In general, female flamingos tend to have purer, more tonal calls, while males utter buzzier, more repetitive vocalizations.[17]

The calls appear to play an integral role in mate–mate and possibly parent–offspring recognition. The size and activity of flamingo colonies should make it difficult for individuals to locate each other by sight *or* sound. However, among greater flamingos at least, it appears that a 'nasal double honk' call is used to facilitate reunions between separated mates. Birds' identities seem to be encoded primarily in the frequency (that is, pitch) characteristics of their honks, though to some extent temporal variations are also important. These two types of traits are probably influenced by vocal cord anatomy, which varies slightly from one bird to the next, thus producing unique vocal signatures. Even though individual flamingos have distinctive voices, however, all birds within a species tend to share vocalizations in the same way that English-speaking humans share the same recognizable words and phrases. The most diverse class of vocalization appears to be alert calling: American flamingos, for example, are known to have repertoires of up to a dozen different vocalizations that allow them to signal to flock-mates that they are alert and suspicious.[18] The naturalist Abel Chapman has vividly described the production of similar calls by greater flamingos:

> on approaching them, which can only be done by extreme caution, their silence is first broken by the sentries, who commence walking away with low croaks; then the whole five hundred necks rise at once to the full extent, every bird gaggling his loudest as they walk obliquely away.[19]

Flamingos' visual signals have been studied in much greater detail than their acoustic signals – partly because they are just too extravagant to ignore.[20] In addition to producing individual-level signals such as those associated with aggression or alarm, some species of flamingo gather in groups of dozens to thousands of birds to perform coordinated displays that appear to be an integral component of the breeding process. These displays, known as marches, are seen in all six species, but are particularly graceful and well-coordinated in the three deep-keeled flamingos (Andean, puna and lesser). Marching displays are initiated when a group of birds gathers into a tightly packed mass in which each bird has its chest pressed up against the back of another.

With necks held high and heads tilted slightly back, the flamingos 'quick-step' first in one direction, then suddenly switch direction and go back the opposite way.

Throughout the march, which can last several minutes, flamingos usually also perform 'head-flagging'. This involves stiffly and repeatedly turning the bill from side to side. Some birds may also perform a 'broken-neck' display, in which the head is brought downward so the bill touches the lower part of the throat. Among American flamingos only, an additional embellishment is 'false-feeding', where birds lean forward while marching, and appear to make 'chomping movements' with their bills. Whatever its final format, marching appears to be a method of coordinating breeding efforts across an entire flock by making sure that all the birds are in the right mood at the right time. Although scientists originally thought that flamingos

Lesser flamingos marching.

have high mate fidelity, recent studies have shown that, among greater flamingos at least, birds are often only monogamous for the course of a single breeding attempt.[21] Thus participation in group displays appears to be an important way to advertise availability and meet potential mates; pairs have often been observed leaving the marching group together.

Several other ritualized movements may be used to promote group cohesiveness. These additional movements may either occur in conjunction with marching performances, or may replace them in species that do not perform the elaborate courtship dances. For example, all six species perform a version of the 'wing salute', which often follows head-flagging. While keeping their bills pointed forward, flamingos spread their scapulars, cock their tails and open their wings before quickly snapping them shut. This displays the vivid red and black of the birds' wing feathers – a sight that is particularly striking in flocks of paler pink birds. According to Abel Chapman, 'a more beautiful sight cannot be imagined than the simultaneous spreading of their thousand crimson wings, flashing against the sky like a gleam of rosy light'.[22] Other displays include the 'twist-preen', the 'inverted wing salute' and the 'wing-leg stretch', each of which is common to different subgroups of the flamingo family. Researchers suspect that these ritualized displays are simply stiffer, exaggerated and more contagious derivatives of 'comfort positions and postures associated with normal behaviour' – though why these developed into socially meaningful movements is still anybody's guess.[23]

Flamingos use many other postural signals to communicate with their flock-mates. Common to all species is the 'alert posture', during which birds stand up straight and extend their necks completely while keeping the bill in a horizontal position and looking back and forth and from side to side. This position often indicates that the birds are suspicious or aware of a source of danger, but are unable to locate it. In *Phoenicopterus* species and the lesser flamingo, birds that are approached by an intruder may perform 'hooking', which is similar to the 'broken-neck' display except that it is accompanied by erection of the scapulars and is held while the disturbed bird walks pointedly towards the offending animal. If this is not sufficient to frighten off the

An American flamingo performing a wing salute.

intruder, the display may escalate into a 'neck-swaying threat', where the neck is extended parallel to the ground while the bill is slightly gaped and pointed toward the focal animal; this is also often accompanied by 'chrysanthemumming' – erection of the scapular feathers in a manner reminiscent of the many-petalled flower – as well as the production of grunting calls. Should all of this posturing fail to impress, birds may engage in actual sparring contests, during which they perform neck-swaying threats towards each other. While these rarely result in serious bodily harm, the birds can push each other over and pull out each other's feathers.

One of the best places to observe this diversity of behaviours is a flamingo colony, a destination that African adventurer George Kirby Yeates referred to as an El Dorado for ornithologists. It took Yeates years of searching before he was able to finally see a 'flamingo city' first-hand; he described it as resembling 'a gigantic and symmetrical flower-bed of huge pink geraniums on red stalks'.[24] Colonies can be massive, consisting of hundreds of thousands of pairs nesting simultaneously. Particularly well-studied colonies – or *pajareras* (nurseries), to use Chapman's term – include those of greater flamingos in the Camargue and Fuente de Piedra Lagoon, American flamingos in several wet-lands across Mexico's Yucatán Peninsula, and lesser flamingos at Lake Natron. At the other end of the spectrum are the South American species, some of whose breeding colonies likely remain undiscovered. Researchers recently estimated that the millions of flamingos distributed around the world cumulatively utilize fewer than 30 nesting sites.[25]

Overall, flamingo breeding efforts can be summarized by just one word: erratic. Although the birds clearly have preferred breeding colonies that have been used repeatedly for countless generations, these are only suitable within a narrow range of

A fight between two pairs of American flamingos – three of which have erected their feathers in the 'chrysanthemum' display.

weather conditions. If there is too little rain, there may not be enough mud to build nests or enough food resources to feed both adults and their chicks. If there is too much rain, nests can be flooded or washed away, and the diluted standing water supply may no longer be saline enough to support the flamingos' preferred prey species. Additionally, flamingos are unwilling to breed unless their flocks obtain a critical mass. Breeding has rarely been observed in groups of fewer than ten flamingos, and then only in captivity; birds perform breeding displays more often and more synchronously in larger flocks in which size remains consistent over time.[26] Further, breeding displays are more likely to lead to successful copulation when performed by larger groups of birds. Thus a fortuitous combination of appropriate weather and simultaneous occupation of the same habitat appears necessary for flamingos to even entertain thoughts of reproduction.

In temperate climates, springtime increases in day length result in hormone fluctuations that cause flamingos to initiate breeding activities. In tropical areas, where there is less variation in day length throughout the year, timing of reproduction is influenced more by the availability of appropriate habitat – a factor determined primarily by weather in general, and by rainfall in particular. All species locate their breeding colonies either within or next to vast areas of shallow saline water, which offers both food and protection from terrestrial predators. Additionally, the mating act itself usually occurs in the water. The female walks forward slowly while mock-feeding, and her potential partner follows closely behind with his chest against her tail and his head positioned over her body. Once the female decides that the time is right for romance, she stands in place and raises her wing tips; with her back and wings, she creates a platform on which the male can balance. If the male is interested in copulation, he will flap his wings and mount the female, exiting forward over her head when he is finished. Observations of terrestrial matings have revealed that female flamingos support the full weight of their partners during these endeavours.[27] Although there are no strict rules governing the timing of the mating act, it is most common in the morning, after the birds have finished their first feeding bout of the day.

In the wild, nest-building efforts also occur primarily in the morning; some captive birds are more active around lunchtime. Females choose an appropriate site and stand in place to indicate where the nest should be built. Both birds in a pair contribute to nest construction, though their activities are generally not co-ordinated despite being simultaneous. Bills are used to scoop mud into a pile between the birds' feet, after which both bills and feet are used to create the final mound shape. Because mud is collected in a circular fashion around the emerging nest mound, a ring-shaped moat is often created around the nest. Sometimes a nest-mate will offer assistance by placing approved materials within reach of its partner. Measurements of old nests reveal that each structure may weigh up to 80 kg (180 lb), suggesting that each pair may excavate 300 kg (660 lb) of mud per nest. The bulk of nests are 30–40 cm (12–15 in.) high and 40–50 cm (15–20 in.) in diameter at the base, tapering to approximately 20 cm (8 in.) at the top. A 2–4 cm (1–2 in.) depression is made at the peak of the nest in order to accommodate the egg. Temperatures in the depression may be up to 8°C (46°F) cooler than in surrounding areas, which is particularly beneficial in East African colonies, where temperatures may reach 50°C (122°F) during the day.[28]

American flamingos incubating eggs at WWT Slimbridge, Gloucestershire.

Each female produces only one egg per nesting attempt; although there have been a few reports of multi-egg nests, these are likely the result of secondary nesting attempts or joint nest occupation by two females. Egg-laying may take as long as an

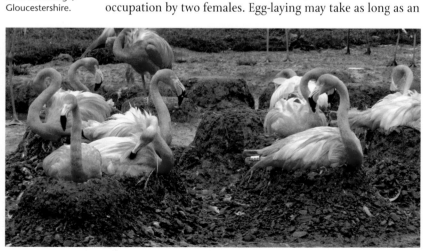

A hatching flamingo chick peeking out of its egg.

hour and requires a bit of finesse: as the egg comes out, the female must lean forward to make sure that it lands within the nest rather than rolling over the edge. Even if addling or break-age could be avoided during such a mishap, it would still end in disaster, since flamingos do not show egg-retrieval behaviours. When such catastrophes occur, pairs are known to make a second or, if necessary, even a third nesting attempt. Among captive flamingos, some unsuccessful pairs (including some in which the birds are of the same sex) have been observed adopting chicks abandoned by other birds; the availability of this alternative breeding option could be why flamingos have not developed a stronger egg-retrieval instinct.[29]

A newly hatched flamingo chick sitting on the remnants of its shell.

The eggs are off-white or very pale blue and are covered in a thick chalky layer. Depending on the species, eggs range in size from 8 × 5 cm (3 × 2 in.) to 9 × 5.5 cm (3.5 × 2 in.) and weigh 115–40 g (4–5 oz). Contrary to some early beliefs that flamingo eggs need only the heat of the sun to develop and eventually hatch,[30] adults must incubate their gestating chicks for approximately one month. Although this duty is shared by both parents, females usually spend more time on the nest. Neither bird, however, has a brood patch (a portion of the belly where feathers have been removed in order to improve heat transfer between parent and egg). When it comes time to hand over incubation duties – something that commonly happens at night – mates make the transition smoothly by leaving and entering the nest from opposite sides. Entry is accompanied by a leg-shaking routine probably designed to rid the feet of excess mud, thereby keeping the nest as clean as possible. Incubating birds have been described as 'restless', frequently standing up, stretching, preening and shifting the egg over the course of an incubation session.

In 1697, the explorer William Dampier wrote in his *A New Voyage Round the World* that incubating flamingos

stand all the while, not on the hillock but close by it with their legs on the ground and in the water, resting themselves against the hillock and covering the hollow nest upon it with their rumps: for their legs are very long; and building thus, as they do, upon the ground, they could

A lesser flamingo parent checks on its young chick.

neither draw their legs conveniently into their nests, nor sit down upon them otherwise than by resting their whole bodies there, to the prejudice of their eggs or their young, were it not for this admirable contrivance which they have by natural instinct.[31]

In other words, to paraphrase Buffon, Dampier thought that flamingos sat upon their nests as humans sit on stools. Another even sillier suggestion was that the birds rested with their legs stuck straight out behind them. Not until 1880 were these theories discredited by the explorer Sir Harry Johnston, who described how flamingos fold their legs under their bellies, as do other incubating birds. A later observer stated that this position made the birds' legs look 'exactly like a couple of sticks of rhubarb'.[32]

Hatching takes as long as 36 hours after the first hole appears in the eggshell. The chicks are precocial, which means that they can if necessary leave the nest and swim within a few hours of hatching. Young flamingos are a greyish white colour, with legs that turn from red to black after about one week, and dark brown-black bills. The latter do not show the characteristic flamingo bend until the birds are about 40 days old, and are not fully developed for filter-feeding until 70–80 days. Unusually among birds, flamingo chicks moult twice; their first downy plumage is replaced by a second at about four weeks post-hatching, and this is followed one to two weeks later by a second moult into juvenile plumage.

Researchers have roughly divided the chick maturation process into six categories.[33] The first two are 'after hatching' and 'standing', which cover the first six days of the chicks' lives and occur while the young are confined to the nest. Because of their relative weakness during this period, chicks often rest in an awkward position in which their legs and feet are stretched out in front of them; this signals the chicks' desire to be brooded by their parents. Although very young birds may initially sit under their parents during brooding, older chicks will tuck themselves under a parent's wing, where they can draw warmth from the adult's body and also place themselves in a good position to be fed. 'Walking' typically begins between days seven and nine, followed by 'exploring' between days ten and twelve. According to the expert Leslie Brown, mobile chicks may bump into eggs and younger birds, potentially causing them harm.[34] Exploration may also have personal costs, since it often takes young birds into the harsh soda water near their nests. As this water evaporates from the chicks' legs, it can leave behind soda rings that can become quite thick and impede movement.

From approximately day thirteen onwards, the adults are increasingly less attentive toward their young. This begins with

After they have grown sufficiently large and independent, juvenile flamingos (greyish) will begin to mix with adults (pinkish).

a period of 'neglect' from days thirteen to fifteen, prompting the young to band together into crèches, or groups of young birds. Although crèches may originally comprise only a few dozen chicks (microcrèches), they eventually swell in size to several hundred chicks (macrocrèches) and, eventually, all the chicks from an entire colony (unique crèche). Flamingo crèches can typically be found in areas of the colony with fewer breeding birds; this works to prevent the chicks suffering aggression from non-parent adults.

Until chicks are capable of gathering their own food, they must rely on their parents for nutrition. Adult flamingos provide chicks with a red substance often inaccurately described as crop milk. In reality, this high-fat, high-protein liquid is secreted by glands in the upper digestive tract. The colour is caused by the pigment canthaxanthin, as well as a small quantity of red blood cells. Parents access the secretion by shaking their heads and wriggling their tongues. A feeding adult will hold its bill above its chick, allowing the fluid to flow down the hooked tip of the beak and into its chick's gaped mouth. Feeding is performed every 45–90 minutes when the young are less than a week old, but becomes less regular as they age; parents of older chicks will actively evade their young, sometimes even running away. 'Weaning' is usually completed, and therefore full independence achieved, by the time the chicks are 60–75 days old.

There are a variety of post-copulation dangers that may reduce reproductive success among flamingos. Nesting birds are incredibly sensitive to disturbance and may abandon colonies *en masse* when approached by potential predators such as humans, gulls and storks. Black-headed gulls (*Chroicocephalus ridibundus*) have been known to pull incubating flamingos off their nests in order to feast on the exposed eggs; unattended eggs and young chicks are also susceptible to these voracious predators. Luckily, flamingos are so long-lived that adults only need to successfully reproduce once every half-dozen years or so in order to sustain their populations.

Breeding has been observed in flamingos (particularly females) as young as two years old, but becomes more likely with increasing age. It is not uncommon for a bird's first few nesting attempts

An American flamingo feeding its chick.

to result in failure. However, once flamingos reach approximately ten years of age, they are much more likely to produce young; the most successful reproducers, at least in captivity, are those in their twenties.[35]

Young flamingos that successfully fledge may have as high as a 70 per cent chance of surviving through their first year, after which their odds of surviving go up to 90 per cent. Full-grown adults are even better off, with an annual survival rate of approximately 95 per cent. Thanks to these odds, flamingos have impressively long lifespans. A greater flamingo at Australia's Adelaide Zoo lived to be 83 years old, and the single surviving puna flamingo at the Slimbridge Wildfowl & Wetlands Trust is thought to be well into his seventies. The longest-lived wild bird on record, a lesser flamingo whose body was recovered at Lake Bogoria (Kenya), was at least 51 years old when it died in the summer of 2013.[36] Judging from participation of captive fiftysomethings in breeding efforts, wild flamingos may continue to reproduce until the very end of their lives. However, this is something the birds do at their own risk: at least one aviculturist reports that it is not uncommon to find older flamingos – especially males – that have died of heart failure mid-copulation.

Health issues in wild birds have been documented primarily in lesser flamingos, which have suffered die-offs caused by infections such as pneumonia and tuberculosis. All species of flamingo are at risk of ingesting neurotoxins produced by water-dwelling microorganisms. In the autumn of 2012, for example, an accumulation of domoic acid from phytoplankton was responsible for the deaths of over 100 greater flamingos and avocets in Namibia.[37] During conditions of low food availability, birds may suffer malnutrition, which can exacerbate immune challenges. Several researchers have postulated that both species of Rift Valley flamingos might be exposed to high levels of metal contamination resulting from industrial run-off; however, research to date indicates that algal blooms and bacterial infections are a bigger threat. Foot maladies are fairly common in captive flamingos, and while these were originally thought to be caused by walking on rough terrain, recent work has revealed that they may actually result from exposure to overly acidic water in the birds' wading pools. Captive chicks also occasionally suffer from a rickets-like malady that leaves them with bent leg bones.

Sadly, the major threat to flamingos is habitat loss caused by anthropogenic disturbances such as soda extraction and construction; nesting failure as a result of human intrusions (by land, water and air) can also reduce population viability. Many flamingo habitats are so remote that the birds are unchallenged by natural predators. Elsewhere, both adults and young are targeted by a variety of species. Probably the most common of these is the marabou stork (*Leptoptilos crumeniferus*), which attacks lesser flamingos so frequently that this behaviour is depicted in the stork's identification plate in many ornithological field guides.[38] Other avian predators include marsh harriers and tawny eagles. Terrestrial predators, which are generally less problematic, include canines (foxes, jackals, hyenas), felines (lions, leopards, cheetahs, jaguars) and feral pigs (in the Galapagos).

2 Flamingos in the Early Human Consciousness

If the cultural importance of a particular species were related to its abundance, then we would certainly expect flamingos to feature extensively in the beliefs and practices of peoples around the world. These bright and personable birds, however, have somehow managed to be cultural wallflowers for the bulk of human history. This likely stems predominantly from the birds' choices of habitat – areas that are generally remote, harsh and hazardous to human visitors. Until the invention of protective walking boots, all-terrain vehicles and aerial transportation, it was often difficult for humans to get more than the briefest or most distant glimpses of flamingos, though of course the birds could be seen flying overhead or, occasionally, feeding in nearby bodies of water. It is thanks to these infrequent events that we do have a few examples of flamingo-themed artwork dating back thousands of years. Since that time, flamingos have gradually worked their way into an increasing number of practices, beliefs, decorations and other cultural products of many groups around the world.

Tracking down 'genuine' flamingo occurrences can sometimes be difficult thanks to a surprising number of mislabelled avian artefacts. Particularly common is the propensity to confuse flamingos with a similarly coloured waterbird, the roseate spoonbill (*Platalea ajaja*). Even non-pink waterbirds are sometimes mistaken

Flamingos at Lake Nakuru, Kenya, stay well away from two predatory marabou storks.

Roseate spoonbills like this one are often mistaken for flamingos.

for flamingos – often because they have comparably long legs and a similar habitat. For example, experts have questioned the accuracy of descriptions applied to several pieces of Moche pottery in a prominent South American museum; the birds painted on these pieces have long, straight bills, suggesting that they were actually meant to represent egrets or herons.[1] Likewise, a fifth-century mosaic from the Church of the Multiplication of the Loaves and Fishes at Tabgha, Israel, has been described as showing a flamingo eating a snake despite the fact that the bird in question is fairly obviously a crane.[2] More bizarre is an academic paper from 1975 in which an art historian describes a 'flamingo' sculpture on Gaudí's Sagrada Família cathedral in Barcelona.[3] The bird actually appears to be a cormorant – a species that is smaller and darker than the flamingo, and lacks the characteristic long legs, hooked bill and filter-feeding habits.

Mistakes are not always visual. For example, in his book *The Mythology of the Wichita*, the American ethnographer George A. Dorsey wrote about a Wichita myth called 'The Man Who Became a Flamingo'.[4] The transformation took place after the main character vowed never to leave the bank of the river in which his young son had disappeared, thus earning him the name Hakeikouwi, or 'Stick-standing-on-the-bank'. Dorsey translates this as 'flamingo', but modern linguistics experts believe the term more accurately describes another waterbird, perhaps a crane or heron – both of which the Wichita encountered relatively frequently.[5] A similar translation error may be responsible for misinterpretation of the Sanskrit term *hamsa*, which definitely

Mosaic dating from the 5th century, from the Church of the Multiplication of the Loaves and Fishes in Tabgha, Israel. Although this bird has been referred to as a flamingo, it is more likely a crane.

A phoenix, as represented in the Aberdeen Bestiary, c. 12th century.

means 'goose' but has also been translated – predominantly by Western researchers – as 'swan' or 'flamingo'. At least one linguist has suggested that the latter two interpretations are favoured in the West because they refer to birds that are considered more elegant and poetic.[6] An examination of the ornithological records reveals that many Sanskrit writers described the presence of *hamsa* in locations where only geese would have been found, making it highly unlikely that this word was ever used to refer to flamingos.

One word that perhaps should be associated with the pink birds – though it rarely is – is 'phoenix'. This mythical firebird can trace its origins to the ancient Egyptians, whose hieroglyphics depict the creature as a grey heron and associate the bird with a word meaning 'rise' or 'shine'.[7] Indeed, the phoenix was linked to the sun god Ra, and was connected with the rising and setting of the sun. In the fifth century CE, the Greek historian Herodotus described the phoenix based on a painting he had seen: 'I can tell you something about the phoenix's size and qualities, namely that its feathers are partly gold but mostly red, and that in appearance and size it is most like an eagle.'[8] Thus the Egyptians appear to have at least occasionally thought of the phoenix as being red rather than grey. While greater flamingos are the palest of the six flamingo species, they do indeed have bold flashes of red on their wings, and their size – or, at least, their wingspan – is not unlike that of an eagle. As mentioned earlier, however, the Greek word *phoinix* refers to the colour red, raising the possibility that our modern interpretation of the phoenix as a crimson bird may result from a misinterpretation of the Greek language. Nevertheless, the birds share at least two other features: their ability to fly, and a propensity to breed under rather extreme circumstances. Just as the phoenix was said to be reborn from flames, either in the form of an egg or as a young bird, so, too, is flamingo breeding conducted in habitats that are hot and forbidding. In fact, descriptions of the phoenix's self-(re)generation call to mind the beliefs of some East African native peoples who used to think that flamingos emerged from the salt pans fully formed;[9] this idea is thought to have arisen from the fact that both nests and chicks were difficult to find and see. Birds in these hot areas would have made quite a dramatic and impressive vision, winging their way out of the salt pans amid the rippling heat waves, seemingly born of nothing but sun and soil. In fact, flamingo biologist Robert Porter Allen writes that early Christians were so impressed by this sight – in particular the cross shape formed by the birds' outstretched wings, neck and legs – that they are responsible for cementing the flamingo-phoenix construct.[10]

Although these relationships might (justifiably) be deemed a bit too tenuous to allow any solid conclusions to be drawn, flamingos have been linked with the phoenix on more than one occasion. In fact, the apparent resemblance between these two birds was supposedly enough to allow the ancient Phoenicians to successfully trade flamingo skins with the Dutch (for amber) and Cornish (for tin), all the while claiming that the skins were those of the mythical firebird. Given how quickly the colour fades from flamingo feathers once they have been removed from their original owners, the Phoenicians must have been very persuasive – or their target audiences very gullible.[11]

Adding complexity to the story of flamingos is the fact that a number of non-phoenicopter objects have been named after flamingos over the past several centuries. One of the earliest of these was the constellation Grus (the Latin word for 'crane'). In seventeenth-century Britain, some people referred to this as Phoenicopterus – understandably, given the long-necked bird shape made by the ten major stars in the constellation. There are also at least seven plants named after the pink birds, including the flamingo lily (*Anthurium andreanum*), a popular houseplant. Two of the most unexpected flamingo namesakes are the flamingo cadherin, a type of protein found in the neural cells of fruit flies, and the flamingo manoeuvre, a complex series of movements that can be performed by a troupe of synchronized swimmers.

Cave paintings are often the medium in which bird species make their first appearances in human cultures, and this is certainly true of flamingos. While some of the most ancient avian cave art was created some 40,000 years ago, the oldest flamingo drawing dates back only 5,000 years.[12] This Neolithic image, painted in the Cueva del Tajo de las Figuras cave in the

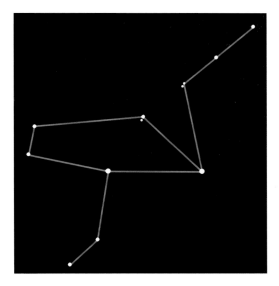

The constellation Grus, which is named after a crane but could easily be mistaken for a flamingo.

An *Anthurium*, known by the common name 'flamingo flower' or 'flamingo lily'.

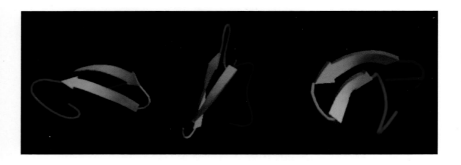

Three views of a flamingo cadherin.

Sierra Momia region of Spain, depicts a single flamingo standing alongside a host of other waterbirds.[13] Given that a large portion of cave art worldwide is devoted to edible species, the flamingo's appearance at the Spanish site may indicate that these birds were occasionally eaten by early humans. There are also theories that some animals were depicted because of their religious significance, or even just because they were frequently encountered near human settlements.[14] It is not easy to explain what led to the flamingo's inclusion in this particular avian tableau – though it is hard not to suspect that early humans might simply have been as impressed and inspired by the flamingo's unique appearance as we are today.

The birds' next known appearance occurs approximately 2,000 years later in ancient Egypt, where flamingos were used in hieroglyphic form both to reference the birds themselves and to indicate the colour red (or, more literally, 'flamingo-coloured').[15] There is some evidence that early Egyptians may have kept flamingos in captivity, though it is not clear whether this was for aesthetic or culinary purposes. The latter is certainly possible given that Egyptians were known to hunt and eat the birds.[16] Indeed, amid the hunting and fishing scenes decorating the Sixth Dynasty (c. 2345–2181 BCE) Tomb of Mehu is the phrase 'Fetch, you who are with me, the flamingo cage!' This presumably refers to a contraption used to capture wild birds, though researchers are not clear on whether 'flamingo' here refers to a phoenicopter or to any similarly sized bird.[17] Other flamingo appearances are less ambiguous. The birds have been found on both pots and reliefs, where their crooked bills and well-preserved colouring leave no doubt about their identity.[18] Particularly noteworthy is a relief at the Fourth Dynasty (*c.* 2613–2494 BCE) tomb of Rahotep, featuring a flock of flamingos with white bodies, red wings and black-tipped beaks.

The Scottish anthropologist James George Frazer reported that flamingos are also important to another eastern African group, the Shilluks, who live along the White Nile in what is now South Sudan. Frazer, writing in 1918, reported that flamingos play an integral role in the Shilluk creation story, which presumably dates back to antiquity. According to the tale, the Creator fashioned each human race out of different colours of mud, then gave

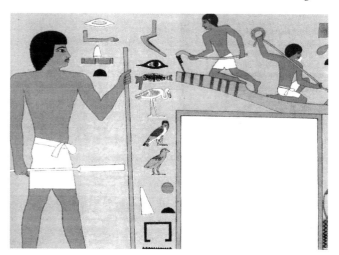

The hieroglyph meaning 'flamingo' and 'red' is the fourth symbol down in the central column in this tomb painting, discovered during a 19th-century excavation of the Medum cemetery in Egypt.

This predynastic (before 3100 BCE) Egyptian pot features a row of flamingos near its base.

people the gift of mobility by fitting them with legs modelled after those of the flamingo.[19]

Elsewhere, the image of flamingos was used in a very different way. In the introduction to *Flamingos*, the definitive flamingo monograph, the late Sir Peter Scott describes a third-century BCE bronze saddle mount found at Brno-Maloměřice in the Czech Republic. Made in the Celtic style, the mount is decorated 'with what is surely a flamingo head'.[20] Unfortunately, Scott does not provide any citations for this information, and so it is impossible to ascertain whether the mount truly does depict a flamingo or simply another bird with a long neck and curved bill. We can, however, confirm references to flamingos made by ancient Greeks living in this same era. The Greeks were familiar with flamingos partly from experiences in their own lands and partly from encounters on Egyptian soil. Writers such as Cratinus, Cleitarchus, Menippus and Aristophanes all mention the birds, sometimes as a feature of the habitat and sometimes as a potential food item. Flamingos premiered onstage in 414 BCE during a performance of Aristophanes' *The Birds*, which follows Pisthetaerus as he convinces the title characters to build a new city in the sky. At the beginning of the play, Pisthetaerus and his friend Euelpides encounter Tereus, once a man and now a hoopoe, who introduces them to the many avian species that appear throughout the story. Tereus calls in a flamingo by imitating its cry, 'toro-toro toro-toro-tix':

Sketch of a 3rd-century Celtic bronze saddle mount found in the Czech Republic.

> BIRD [offstage]: Toro-tix, toro-tix.
> PISTHETAERUS: Hey, my good man, here comes a bird.
> [Enter a flamingo, very tall and flaming red – something Pisthetaerus and Euelpides have never seen]
> EUELPIDES: By Zeus, that's a bird? What kind would you call that? It couldn't be a peacock, could it?
> [Tereus re-enters from the thicket]
> PISTHETAERUS: Tereus here will tell us. Hey, my friend, what's that bird there?
> TEREUS: Not your everyday fowl – the kind you always see. She's a marsh bird.
> EUELPIDES: My goodness, she's gorgeous – flaming red!
> TEREUS: Naturally, that's why she's called Flamingo.[21]

Flamingo biologist Robert Porter Allen considers this passage remarkable because, 'even at such an early date, we have identification, including field marks, a description of the voice (albeit

An elderly fisherman straining to draw up a net while watched by three men, with a flamingo on the left; illustration for the *Arabian Nights*, 1865.

with a large share of poetic license), a description of the habitat, [and] an outspoken aesthetic appreciation'.[22]

A flamingo also makes a brief appearance in Heliodorus of Emesa's *Aethiopica* of the third century CE, in which the author describes flamingos as birds of the Nile and has one of his characters race to fetch one in an attempt to woo a woman. During his trip home, the man encounters his friend Nausicles, who says: 'How easy a lover you have gotten . . . and how light be her commands, when she bids you get her a flamingo and not rather a phoenix, which bird cometh to us from the Ethiopians and the men of Ind.'[23] This passage is interesting not only for its suggestion that a flamingo might be considered an appropriate gift in a romantic context – probably because of the difficulty associated with its capture as much as with its beauty and edibility – but also for the clear distinction made between this undoubtedly real species and the legendary phoenix.

The Greeks were also responsible for the only known mention of flamingos in Judaeo-Christian religious texts. This is found in the Septuagint Bible (also known as the LXX or Greek Old Testament), a document that is thought to have been created between the third and first centuries BCE by 72 Jewish scholars working at the behest of King Ptolemy.[24] Charles Thomson, secretary of the American Continental Congress, translated the Bible in the eighteenth century and specifically listed flamingos among the many 'birds of abomination' described in Leviticus (11:13–19). *Anafah*, the original Hebrew word used in this section, translates as 'big noselike beak', which is generally thought to refer to herons rather than their pink cousins. However, while herons' bills are undeniably 'big', they are much less 'noselike' than the hooked beaks of flamingos. Further, *anafah* are named in a category listing birds with 'wide white wings edged with black' – a description that, again, fits flamingos better than herons. Bible scholar Virginia C. Holmgren, however, believes that *anafah* applies equally to both herons and flamingos, thus rendering them both off-limits.[25]

Unlike their Jewish neighbours, the Romans had absolutely no qualms about eating flamingos; they were so fond of the birds that some of them even decorated their homes with mosaics showing flamingos being prepared for food. Indeed, the clergyman George Hakewill would later write that 'The fowle which [the Romans] specially hunted after and most delighted in, were Phoenicopters, Peacockes, Thrushes, and Pigeons.'[26] What he neglects to mention is that the Romans were particularly fond of the birds' tongues, and considered them a great delicacy. This

tradition may have begun with the first-century CE gourmand Marcus Gavius Apicius who, says Robert Porter Allen, 'introduced the thick, oily tongue of the flamingo, properly pickled, as a delicacy without which no Roman banquet was really of the first class'.[27] Not long after, Vitellius – who served as Roman emperor for only a few months in 69 CE – created a dish he referred to as

> the Shield of Minerva, Defender of the City. In this, he mingled the livers of pike, the brains of pheasants and peacocks, the tongues of flamingoes and the milt of lampreys, brought by his captains and triremes from the whole empire, from Parthia to the Spanish strait.[28]

Vitellius' excesses – which were hardly limited to the culinary realm – were recorded by Suetonius in his *De vita Caesarum*, also known as *On the Life of the Caesars* or, more commonly, *The Twelve Caesars*. Even more excessive than Vitellius, however, was Caligula, whose earlier reign (37–41 CE) was also chronicled by Suetonius.

According to the biographer, flamingos were only one of the many birds that rich citizens sacrificed in the temple that Caligula established in his own honour. The emperor also sacrificed birds to the gods, and in fact was sprayed by the blood of one unfortunate flamingo on the very day that he was assassinated. Caligula's murder had previously been predicted by a variety of seers, and so many regarded the flamingo's blood as an ill omen; if only Caligula had shared their belief and been more cautious, perhaps he might have avoided being stabbed later that afternoon.[29]

Despite these grisly tales, Lampridius reports that flamingo was still in vogue in Rome over a century later, when the bird was served at a banquet by the decadent young emperor Heliogabalus, who reigned from 218–22 CE. In his *Natural History of Birds*, the Comte de Buffon writes that Heliogabalus supplied his guests with platters of flamingo tongues; more modern translations have indicated that it was instead the birds' brains that were eaten.[30] Buffon also quotes several more recent flamingo connoisseurs who variously describe the bird as tasting 'pretty good', having flesh as delicate as that of a partridge, being lean and 'slightly marshy', and ranking 'among the delicacies of entertainments'. The poet Martial, disgusted by the gluttony evidenced by his emperors, questioned whether flamingos might have been spared if they not only looked beautiful, but could also produce a delightful song.[31] Martial also describes how flamingos were fattened at Baiae, indicating that, like the Egyptians, Romans may have been keeping the pink birds in captivity.

One reason why the Romans may have indulged in such dietary excess was that Aulus Cornelius Celsus, first-century BCE author of *De Medicina*, had recommended flamingos as a nourishing food that was 'of general assistance not only in diseases of all kinds but in preserving health as well'.[32] Specifically, he believed that flamingos were one of many avian species in the 'middle class' of foods – those that were more wholesome than fruits, shellfish and vegetable stalks, but not quite as healthy as honey, cheese or pulses. *Apicius*, or *De re coquinaria*, a fourth- or fifth-century Roman cookbook compiled by Caelius Apicius (not, as you might expect, the aforementioned Marcus Gavius Apicius), provide detailed instructions for preparing flamingo. The recipe was later quoted in a footnote by the Comte de Buffon:

> Cleanse, wash, and truss the phoenicopterus; put it into a kettle; add water, salt, and a little vinegar. At half boiling, tie in it a bunch of leeks and coriander, that it may stew: near boiling, drop into it spiced wine, and colour the mixture. Put into a mortar pepper, cummin, coriander, the root of laser, mint, rue; pound these, pour on vinegar, add walnut-date. Pour on it its own gravy, and turn the whole back into the same kettle: close it with starch; pour on the gravy, and carry it in.

Otherwise, *Apicius* recommends that you should

> Roast the bird; grind pepper, loveage, parsley-seeds, sesame, spiced wine, wild parsley, mint, dry onions, walnut-dates; and temper the whole with honey, wine, pickle, vinegar, oil, and spiced wine.[33]

Remarkably, flamingos virtually disappear from Mediterranean and European culture after the third century CE and do not re-emerge for nearly a millennium; neither do the birds make any major appearances in African artefacts. There are, however, a few intriguing 'sightings' elsewhere in the world. In Peru, for instance, one of the Nazca geoglyphs is sometimes referred to as The Flamingo – though it has also been called The

Cormorant, The Stork and The Egret. The glyphs are thought to have been created between 400 and 650 CE and may therefore represent some of, if not the, earliest images of flamingos in the New World.[34] While flamingos have been said to feature in Mayan glyphs and Incan icons, it is hard to find academic treatments of these artefacts, or any proof that the featured birds are not other (more frequently encountered) long-legged waders. However, in his description of Cortés's conquest of Mexico City, the sixteenth-century conquistador Bernal Díaz reports that Moctezuma II (Montezuma) kept flamingos in his menagerie; native Cubans were also reported to have collections of captive flamingos.[35] This suggests that New World cultures may have had a long history of appreciating the pink birds.

Both nineteenth- and twentieth-century ethnographers describe the use of flamingo adornments among New World natives – practices that may have been handed down from one generation to the next and, therefore, likely originate in this 'early flamingo period'. The 1901 edition of *Harper's Encyclopaedia of United States History* states that 'principal people' in the

Flamingo Nazca glyph in Peru.

Creek tribes wore flamingo feathers on their heads. Given that the Creek lived throughout the American Southeast, it is certainly possible that they might have encountered the feathers of American flamingos, either directly or via their southern neighbours.[36] A flamingo-feather headband made by the Yunga people had its origins even further south, on the Bolivian slopes of the Cordillera de los Andes. Collected by the American explorer A. Hyatt Verrill, the piece consists of dozens of feathers tied to llama-wool yarn. Taken together, these items suggest that flamingos were not an uncommon source of craft material in areas where the birds could be found sharing space with humans. Unfortunately, because there are few detailed histories of these tribes' ancient cultural practices, it is difficult to pinpoint when and why these decorative practices might have emerged.

That said, an abundance of records has not done much to decrease levels of uncertainty associated with early Indian references to the pink birds. For example, the 'flamingos' mentioned in the *Upanishads* may actually be geese suffering from a case of mistaken identity, thanks to a mistranslation of the word *hamsa*. It is unclear whether there is a similar issue with a passage from the *Mahabharata* listing the many birds whose feathers Hindu warriors used when crafting arrows. The Sanskrit epic (originating around 400 BCE) mentions that suitable sources of feathers included not only flamingos, but also herons, hawks, osprey, geese, vultures and peacocks; using sinew and thread, the ancient Indians would have fastened four quills to shafts made of reed, wood or bamboo.[37] Interestingly, there is also an early Islamic reference to flamingos within the context of archery: the thirteenth-century poet Safi ad-Din al-Hilli mentions flamingos as one of fourteen *tuyur al-wadijh* (obligatory birds) that crossbow archers needed to kill to earn points during the *futuwwa* (chivalrous competitions for young men) organized by caliph al-Nasir li-Din Allah.[38]

Another fourteenth-century Islamic text attempts to educate readers on flamingo natural history. To his credit, the author, Al-Damiri, does manage to accurately describe the flamingo nest, which he correctly identifies as being made of mud and having a more or less pyramidal shape; beyond that, however, his lack of first-hand observations is telling. He claims, for example, that females are fertilized by 'an oral regurgitation on the part of the male'; once the eggs are laid, Al-Damiri states, the males cover them with their droppings and allow the developing chicks to be incubated by the sun. Finally, he writes that the chicks are effectively stillborn, but that their mothers breathe life into them by performing a sort of beak-to-beak resuscitation. Unsurprisingly, scholars are not sure what to make of Al-Damiri's claims that the prophet Muhammad once ate flamingo. One thing they do know, however, is that Islamic law permits consumption of the birds' flesh. Despite this, it is hard to imagine too many Muslims who would want to eat flamingo meat after reading a transcription of a sermon delivered by the eighth-century imam Ja'far al-Sadiq. The purpose of the oration was to highlight the natural wonders of the world, so as to convince listeners that these magnificent things could not possibly have come into being by chance. During the second of four sessions, the imam focused on remarkable animals, listing sparrows, owls, pheasants, peacocks and – of course – flamingos.[39] Old Islamic texts also indicate that Muslims used flamingos in a variety of medical contexts; sore joints, for instance, were sometimes treated by flamingo-fat ointment or by plasters containing, essentially, liquefied flamingos (obtained by boiling the birds whole for long periods of time), while ear troubles could be cured by the application of pastes made from flamingo tongues. These beliefs are reminiscent of those of Andean miners, who once prized flamingo oil for its (theoretical) ability to cure tuberculosis.[40]

The final 'early' flamingo reference appears to be a comment made by the Mughal emperor Zahir-ud-din Muhammad Babur (1483–1530), noting the presence of the birds on Afghanistan's lake Ab-e Istada.[41] After this time, there is little evidence that flamingos played an important role in Middle and Near Eastern cultures, or even captured the attention of residents in these regions. Not so in the West, where an increasing interest in exploration and colonization soon brought the brilliant-pink birds back into the spotlight.

3 The Rise of the Modern Flamingo

Around the same time that flamingos were seemingly disappearing from Middle Eastern literature and artwork, they began to make a resurgence in the West. John Foxe's *Actes and Monuments* (published in 1563, and also known as Foxe's *Book of Martyrs*) contains the first English-language discussion of the pink birds, which are referred to as 'a straunge fowle called *Phenocapterie*'.[1] The fact that the word 'flamingo' had not yet been invented was soon rectified by the publication in 1589 of Richard Hakluyt's *The Principall Navigations, Voiages and Discoveries of the English Nation*. A portion of Hakluyt's text recounts the experiences of John Sparke, one of many men who voyaged to Florida on a ship commanded by John Hawkins, the first Englishman to navigate northwards up the American coast. During the ship's time in Florida, Sparke caught sight of a number of indigenous bird species:

> Fowles also there be many, both upon land and upon sea: but concerning them on the land I am not able to name them, because my abode there was so short. But for the fowle of the fresh rivers, these two I noted to be the chiefe, whereof the Flemengoas one, having all red feathers, and long red legs like a herne, a necke according to the bill, red, whereof the upper neb hangeth an inch over the nether . . .

Alice and her flamingo croquet mallet, as visualized by Sir John Tenniel in 1865.

Alice and the Duchess during the game of croquet.

This description not only introduced the word 'flamingo' into the English language, but also marked the first time that Europeans made note of New World phoenicopters. Several other travellers – including Thomas Herbert in 1634 and William Dampier in 1697 – also wrote memoirs that included details of their encounters with flamingos.

It was not until the early nineteenth century that flamingos first appeared in literature, in Johann David Wyss's *The Swiss Family Robinson* (1812), where they are mentioned as a source of feathers for arrows. The birds also made an appearance in Honoré de Balzac's *Modeste Mignon* (1844) and Jules Verne's *From the Earth to the Moon* (1865), among other notable works of fiction. Possibly the most famous literary reference to flamingos is in Lewis Carroll's *Alice's Adventures in Wonderland* (1865), in which flamingos are used as croquet mallets. One of the reasons this scene is so well known is that it is not only described in the text, but also depicted in Sir John Tenniel's iconic and beloved illustrations. Carroll had originally selected ostriches to be used as mallets, but switched species prior to his book's widespread publication because flamingo bills had a more appropriate shape – not to mention the fact that they would be much easier for a young girl to lift.[2] However, even this relatively small pink bird gave Alice some trouble:

> The chief difficulty Alice found at first was in managing her flamingo: she succeeded in getting its body tucked away, comfortably enough, under her arm, with its legs hanging down, but generally, just as she had got its neck nicely straightened out, and was going to give the hedge-hog a blow with its head, it would twist itself round and look up in her face, with such a puzzled expression that she could not help bursting out laughing.

Alice certainly does look bemused in Tenniel's illustration, though also slightly melancholy; the flamingo appears to be regarding her with great consternation. This beloved scene has since been re-imagined by countless artists; both their work and Tenniel's original image can be found in a variety of unusual forms, including party favours, tattoos and balloon art. One of the most unexpected homages can be found in the video game *Prince of Persia: Warrior Within*. The game's programmers wanted to create a more modern and deadly version of the flamingo mallet, so they designed a weapon shaped like a plastic lawn flamingo; hidden away in a secret location, this unusual tool can be discovered and wielded only by the most advanced players.[3]

In 1950 the naturalists Étienne Gallet and George Kirby Yeates made flamingo biology more accessible to the public in their popular science books *The Flamingos of the Camargue* and *Flamingo City*, respectively; Leslie Brown's *The Mystery of the Flamingos* followed in 1959. Books like these offer a fascinating insight not only into the life histories of flamingos as they were understood by the first modern flamingo experts, but also the obsessive nature of the fanatical explorers who in some cases nearly killed themselves in their attempts to locate and observe the reclusive pink birds. Malcolm and Carol Ogilvie recount some of these horrific tales in their book *Flamingos* (1984), the last popular press treatment of the phoenicopters. One nightmare journey they describe is a research expedition initiated in the hopes of finding breeding puna flamingos at Bolivia's Laguna Colorada:

> The first island proved to be well over a mile into the lake. The water was shallow, but every so often there were apparently bottomless holes out of which hot water bubbled from volcanic subterranean springs. Stretches of soft slimy mud were interspersed with areas of hard salty crust, through which [the explorers'] feet often broke, gashing their ankles and legs on the sharp edges.[4]

Leslie Brown also notes that flamingo exploration is hard on the feet: ' . . . all flamingo hunters brag about the number of toenails they have lost in the search and I have stopped counting mine'.[5]

Brown and his fellow phoenicopteriphiles would have been much happier visiting flamingos in the habitats described in Jean Ingelow's poem 'Sandmartins' of 1867, which is apparently the first English-language treatment of the birds in verse. Ingelow describes how the eponymous birds 'play / in slumberous azure pools, clear as the air, / where rosy-winged flamingos fish all day'. This is a more light-hearted scene than the one featured in the title poem of Kay Ryan's highly respected volume *Flamingo Watching* (1994); Ryan writes that the pink bird is 'unnatural by nature – / too vivid and peculiar / a structure to be pretty'.[6]

This is a passage that likely resonates with the millions of readers who recently saw media coverage of a graceless Moscow Zoo flamingo that awkwardly flailed about in the water after losing his balance while feeding. Unfortunately for the poor animal, photographer Tatiana Adamenko was standing nearby at the time; within hours, her images of the event were plastered across the Internet. This is but one of the many flamingo news stories that can be found on the Web; the press seem to be very fond of these charismatic and instantly recognizable birds. Readers who get their news online can find flamingo stories covering a range

Graceless flamingo at the Moscow Zoo.

of topics, from results produced by recent flamingo research to popular culture events involving flamingos (for example, use of an inflatable flamingo toy to distract basketball player LeBron James during a game[7]) and updates on the whereabouts of several flamingos that escaped from captivity and proceeded to tour the u.s., uk and Japan.[8]

There are also a number of webpages on which flamingo fans share their love of the pink birds. One of the most informative sites is the Wildfowl & Wetlands Trust's 'Flamingo Diary', written by University of Exeter researcher Paul Rose. The diary was initiated in the spring of 2012 to provide natural history details about each of the Slimbridge facility's six resident species, as well as updates on the birds' breeding activities.[9] Other pages are a bit more tongue-in-cheek. Uncyclopedia – the 'content-free encyclopedia' – has an entry on flamingos in which the birds are described as 'superiorly awesome to anything else that exists, or ever has existed'.[10] Capitalizing on the instant recognizability of the flamingo profile, there are also a number of blogs with a flamingo 'mascot'. One example is April Geiger's 'The Striped Flamingo', which featured a succession of banners sporting flamingos in various postures because the author liked the sense of whimsy the animals lent her site.[11]

A longitudinal survey of modern flamingo writing reveals that whimsy is only one of many ideas associated with the word 'flamingo'. From 1862, the term 'flamingo-legged' was used to evoke the birds' unusual stance. Likewise, a 'flamingo view' X-ray is one taken while the patient takes turns standing on only one leg while keeping the other lifted. The word was first applied in a botanical context in 1882 when *Garden* magazine referred to *Anthurium scherzerianum* as 'the flamingo flower' and 'the flamingo plant'. Although this common name was inspired by the plants' bright coloration, 'flamingo' was not directly used to

refer to a particular hue until the *Westminster Gazette* ran a piece referring to 'poor little flamingo-caped lassies' in June 1897. Since that time, many authors have described various parts of their scenery as being coloured like flamingos; notable examples include Florence Barclay, in *The Rosary* (1909) and Virginia Woolf, in *The Voyage Out* (1915). Now more than ever, the birds also take centre stage as main characters (as in Bob McCreadie's children's book *Fred the Fabulous Flamingo* of 2012) and major plot devices (as in Susan Trott's novel *Flamingo Thief* of 2010). It may have taken nearly 500 years, but flamingos have now firmly established themselves in the English canon.

From the sixteenth century onwards, many adventurers returned from their expeditions with flamingo specimens – both live animals, which could be displayed in zoos and menageries, and skins that could be displayed in curio cabinets. These birds inspired a number of craftsmen to continue the venerable tradition of using flamingos in art and decoration.

The earliest modern flamingo images generally fall into two categories. The first is paintings that happen to feature flamingos as one of many animals in a scene or collection. Though aesthetically appealing, these are often ecologically improbable, and typically relegate flamingos to the background. The great Dutch bird artist Gillis Claesz. d'Hondecoeter, for

example, places a flamingo alongside a turkey, crane, parrot, hoopoe and several species of fowl in his appropriately titled *Various Birds* (late sixteenth/early seventeenth century). Similar scenes are shown in Adriaen van Oolen's *Ornamental Fowl* (seventeenth century), Jakob Bogdani's *Flamingo and Other Birds in a Landscape* (mid-seventeenth/early eighteenth century), Johannes van Bronckhorst's *A Park Landscape with Deer and Exotic Birds* (*c.* 1710) and Philip Reinagle's lengthily titled *A Penguin, a Pair of Flamingoes, and Other Exotic Birds, Shells, and Coral on the Shoreline* (mid-eighteenth/early nineteenth century). The goal of these images was clearly not to provide any biological or scientific information to the viewer, but instead to create a two-dimensional collection of the most visually pleasing animals known at that time.

The other category of flamingo images encompasses the natural history artwork intended to educate viewers about the plumage, anatomy and morphology of the six species of flamingo. Although the creators of these pieces were predominantly focused on accurately depicting their subjects, they were also proficient artists whose work was often quite appealing. One of the earliest

Gillis Claesz. d'Hondecoeter's *Various Birds,* one of many menagerie paintings common between the 17th and 19th centuries.

John White's *A Flaminco*, which portrays an American flamingo seen during White's voyages in the New World, *c.* 1590.

examples of this style is John White's late sixteenth-century drawing *A Flaminco*, one of a series of sketches that White produced during a voyage to the New World. While many of his drawings focused on species that had a practical purpose – as food, for instance – researchers believe that the flamingo was included solely because it was considered unusual and interesting. The historian Kim Sloan reports that ornithologists are particularly appreciative of White's attention to details in the bird's feathering; indeed, the entire rendering is surprisingly accurate and lifelike.[12] Many accomplished and highly respected artists followed in White's footsteps and created their own flamingo renderings; these include Eleazar Albin (presumably an American flamingo, 1741), Mark Catesby (American flamingo,

1754), John Latham ('red flamingo', 1780s), Sarah Stone (American flamingo, 1788), Alexander Wilson (American flamingo, 1832), Edward Lear (greater flamingo, 1832–7) and Coenraad Temminck (greater flamingo, early nineteenth century).[13]

Perhaps the most remarkable natural history portrait is John James Audubon's depiction of a Caribbean flamingo of 1838. What it lacks in biological accuracy, it makes up for in size: the plate used to produce the image for Audubon's groundbreaking *Birds of America* was a massive 97 × 65 cm (38 × 26 in.).[14] By all accounts, this was the largest piece of flamingo art produced at that point in time, and appears to remain the largest rendering of a phoenicopter to this day.

Mark Catesby's American flamingo, *c.* 1731–43.

95

More recent flamingo artwork is less easy to categorize, sometimes blurring the lines between these two earlier genres, and sometimes falling within entirely new classifications. Charley Harper, a twentieth-century wildlife artist famous for his geometric designs, produced a number of flamingo images that reduce the birds to a few simple shapes and yet still manage to capture the essence of the animals as they engage in activities such as incubating, feeding and displaying towards potential mates. An equally informative yet much more disturbing painting by D. W. Makela shows an unfortunate chick that has developed soda rings around its legs and is lying helpless in the water.

Many contemporary artists use more abstract styles and often associate flamingos with dreamscapes and otherworldly scenes. In her eerie 1930 piece *Untitled (Fantastic Landscape)*, Ruth Pershing Uhler painted several ghostly greater flamingos feeding in a moonlit pool in the middle of a dark mangrove swamp. More recently, Kaitlin Beckett's flamingo-machine hybrid was designed as an '"anti-lawn-ornament" version of a flamingo', and was inspired by a nature documentary showing an aggregation of flamingos that the artist perceived as an unpleasant 'squawking sea of pink feathers, demonic red eyes, and hooked black

Charley Harper's *Flamingo-a-go-go*, 1988.

Flamebird, a painting of a Chilean flamingo by Jeremy Paul, 2004.

beaks'.[15] A more light-hearted flamingo piece can be found in Svjetlan Junaković's *Great Book of Animal Portraits* (2007), a humorous and award-winning collection of classic artwork in which humans have been replaced with animals. One portrait was inspired by Bronzino's *Portrait of Laura Battiferri*, originally painted around 1560. Battiferri is shown with a rather prominent nose and somewhat awkwardly splayed fingers; Junaković re-imagines her as a hook-billed flamingo with feathery wingtips.

One of the most unique canvases for modern flamingo artwork is the human body. The painter Gesine Marwedel received international acclaim after an image of her full-size flamingo body art went viral in late 2011. According to the artist, her painting was quite difficult to achieve because her model 'could only stand [in the flamingo pose] for two or three seconds before falling down, and the photographer had to hurry up with taking pictures.'[16] Several other artists, including the Italian painters Mario Mariotti and Guido Daniele, and the British painter Victoria Gugenheim,

Lake Flamingotati, by Kamala Dolphin-Kingsley, 2007.

have created smaller-scale flamingos using only hands and arms; Daniele refers to these creations as 'handimals'.

Flamingos have also been the subject of more conventional three-dimensional pieces. The first modern flamingo sculpture appears to be an elegant bronze statue crafted by Paul Manship in 1932. The Smithsonian's National Museum of the American Indian in Washington, DC, features a delicate cypress wood flamingo carving made by Ingram Billie – a Seminole who is one of only a handful of Native American artists who have produced

Kaitlin Beckett's flamingo from *A Curious Bestiary*, 2010.

Gesine Marwedel's full-body American flamingo body art project, 2011.

American flamingo
hand painting by
Victoria
Gugenheim, 2012.

flamingo-themed work. Probably the most famous phoenicopter sculpture is Alexander Calder's *Flamingo*, unveiled in Chicago in 1974. On permanent display in the Federal Center Plaza at Dearborn and Adams Streets, the installation was the first piece commissioned by the United States General Services

Alexander Calder's *Flamingo*, on display in downtown Chicago since 1974.

Flamingo-shaped gold weight made in Ghana between the 18th and 20th centuries.

Administration's Art in Architecture program. The massive piece is 16 m (53 ft) tall, covers a ground area of 7 × 18 m (24 × 60 ft) and weighs 50 tonnes. *Flamingo* was designed to allow viewers to see it equally well from all angles – above, directly beneath and around its entire perimeter. A maquette version, or scale model, of the statue can be found at the Smithsonian American Art Museum.

The twentieth century also saw flamingos inspiring artists from genres that had never before paid much attention to the birds. In 1940, for example, Ted Grouya wrote the classic jazz standard 'Flamingo', first recorded by Herb Jeffries and Duke Ellington; British pop band Manfred Mann reached the top of the UK music charts in 1966 with their rendition of 'Pretty Flamingo'. The Chicago-based doo-wop group The Flamingos were popular around this same time on the other side of the Atlantic. On the silver screen, phoenicopters were associated with notable films such as *Flamingo Road* (1949), starring Joan Crawford; *Pink Flamingos* (1972), the cult classic by John Waters; and *The Flamingo Kid* (1984), which was later adapted for the small screen. Not surprisingly, flamingos have also played a role in international films set in countries where the pink birds reside; examples include *O último voo do flamingo*, made in Mozambique, and *Flamingo No. 13*, made in Iran (both released in 2010). On the small screen, the birds have made memorable appearances on the U.S. children's show *Sesame Street* (in the character of Plácido Flamingo, an opera-singing bird whose name was a nod to the famous tenor Plácido Domingo) and the animated Canadian series *Captain Flamingo* (in the character of Milo Powell, who transformed into the super-powered title character to save children in need).

Early twentieth-century marketing executives, appreciating flamingos' charisma, cheerful colouring and whimsical physiques,

Early 20th-century bronze flamingo panel.

used phoenicopters in advertising campaigns designed to lighten the hearts of the populace and stimulate economies that had been hard hit by two world wars and the Great Depression. Flamingos were associated with products as varied as textiles, medications, airlines and tickets to zoological gardens – where, to this day, the pink birds are recognized as being one of the most perennially beloved attractions.

Flamingo symbolism was particularly popular among establishments looking to draw in customers by reminding them of the exotic and tropical vacation spots frequented by the social elite – who, in that era, were the only people who could afford to travel to the sorts of warm, tropical habitats where flamingos reside. In the 1930s aspiring socialites could meet up at the Waldorf Astoria's Flamingo Room in order to have a gourmet meal and dance to musical acts such as Michael Zarin and his orchestra. From 1946 onwards, visitors to Las Vegas could try to hit the jackpot at Bugsy Siegel's Flamingo Hotel (reportedly

Iago, sidekick of the main villain, Jafar, in Disney's 1992 hit film *Aladdin*, disguises himself as a flamingo.

Zimmerli Tricots, a Swiss clothing company, used flamingos to advertise their products in the early 20th century.

named after his girlfriend, whose long legs earned her the moniker 'Flamingo'). Over the years, the flamingo motif has been adopted by a number of other hotels, including several that have tried to attract the attention and patronage of passers-by by erecting giant flamingos next to the highway. If nothing else, these big birds have become popular among tourists who enjoy collecting photographs of unusual roadside sculptures.

Other flamingo destinations include several Flamingo Roads, Bays and Lakes, and even a Flamingo Land (in Malton, North Yorkshire), to name but a few. The Dutch Caribbean island of Bonaire is home to a Flamingo International Airport – which, appropriately, is painted pink. Both India and Kazakhstan host annual flamingo festivals. These events celebrate the arrival of breeding flamingos while also raising awareness of avian bio-diversity and encouraging the public to preserve the precious wetlands in which these animals live.[17]

ZIMMERLI TRICOTS

One of many Flamingo motels in the U.S.

South West Africa stamp.

The birds are not only associated with particular locations, but also with several different methods of getting there. In 1876 the British Royal Navy christened their newest composite screw gun-vessel the HMS *Flamingo*,[18] thus beginning a long tradition of naming prominent vehicles after the pink birds. Later flamingo transports include the Flamingo G-2W monoplane (an aeroplane that made headlines for being the model flown by pilot Jimmie Angel when he became the first outsider to view Venezuela's Angel Falls), the de Havilland DH.95 Flamingo monoplane and HMBS *Flamingo* (a ship involved in the only combat action ever seen by the Royal Bahamas Defence Force).[19] The American company Adventureglass even produces a pink flamingo paddleboat.

Other mainstream flamingo appearances are more utilitarian. Several countries, beginning with Russia and Mauritania in 1962, have issued flamingo stamps. There are also a variety of flamingo currencies, including the Bahamian $2 coin of 1971 and the Kazakhstani 500 tenge coin of 2009, both made of silver.

Flamingo International Airport, Kralendijk, Bonaire, Dutch Antilles.

Amazingly, flamingos have also been reintroduced as culinary delicacies – but in name rather than in body. The birds have inspired several alcoholic beverages, including the 'Pink Flamingo Rita' at Cheeseburger in Paradise restaurants, the 'Champagne Flamingo' (a blend of vodka, Campari and chilled champagne) and a number of different Pink Flamingo cocktails with varying recipes but similar coloration. True flamingo aficionados would likely be interested in sipping their beverages from one of the many flamingo-themed mugs and cups on the market; also available are flamingo straws, toothpicks, paper plates, chopsticks, coasters, napkins, tea towels and aprons. Flamingo motifs have become so popular over the last several years that it is also possible to purchase flamingo dolls, jewellery, clothing, costumes, decorative lights, umbrellas, games, puzzles, notepads,

Flamingo paddleboat made by Adventureglass.

Azerbaijan stamp.

Peruvian flag; its red and white colouring is commonly associated with flamingos.

writing implements, wind chimes, stained glass and much, much more. Thanks to this bounty of flamingo-themed merchandise, Floridian Sherry Knight was recently able to earn her place in the *Guinness World Records* by piecing together a collection of 619 separate phoenicopter-related items. This achievement highlights both how beloved and how prevalent flamingo imagery is in contemporary mainstream culture.[20]

To many groups, flamingos are more than just a pretty face; they are also an important emblem or mascot – a symbol to rally behind. Some Peruvians, for instance, claim that the colours of their national flag represent flamingos (red) flying across a cloudy (white) sky. The Bahamas, another country with a large resident population of flamingos, chose the American flamingo as its national bird, and features it prominently on their coat of arms. Flamingos are also the official bird of the Indian state of Gujarat, as well as the mascot of sports teams in Jamaica (football) and the U.S. (cycling, kickball).

Phoenicopters have no official emblematic status for any U.S. states or governmental institutions, but a sword- and shield-wielding flamingo was adopted as the mascot of the United States' 435th Air Ground Operations Wing, which is currently stationed at Ramstein Air Base in Germany. The symbol dates

Sterling silver Bahamian coin decorated with American flamingos, first minted in 1974.

Henry Stacy Marks cabinet with flamingo decoration, c. 1865; Marks also produced conventional paintings of the pink birds.

Bahamas coat of arms, featuring the country's national bird, the American flamingo, 1971.

back to the 1940s, when the wing was stationed in Florida – a much more tropical and flamingo-friendly location. According to the wing's historian, the 435th Fight'n' Flamingo was also an appropriate symbol because, like the pilots it represented, it could fly over long distances. Although the emblem has now

Tea trolley with flamingo motif, by contemporary British designer Lucy Turner – whose studio door is also decorated with a pink flamingo.

Fight'n' Flamingo emblem of the 435th Air Ground Operations Wing stationed at the Ramstein Air Base, Germany, 20th century.

officially been retired, it is still remembered fondly by those stationed at Ramstein.[21]

Flamingos also had a military/political connotation to Nigerian author Bode Sowande, who in 1986 published a play titled *Flamingo*. The plot explores corruption, violence and morality among politicians. 'Flamingo', used synonymously with the phrase 'all flames go', is the code name of an effort to start a coup that will topple a crooked government and replace it with one selected by the people.[22] The brightly coloured birds are an appropriate symbol of the cleansing fire that the characters hope will begin a new era in their country; given flamingos' propensity to aggregate in enormous numbers, they are also a good metaphor for the downtrodden masses leading the revolt depicted in the play.

Sowande's work is clearly intended for adults, but flamingo imagery can also be found in children's literature. One of the best examples is in Horacio Quiroga's story '*Las medias de los flamencos*', or 'The Flamingos' Socks', one of several fables published in Quiroga's book *Cuentos de la selva* (*Jungle Tales*, 1918). The tale explains how flamingos got their brightly coloured legs, as well as why the birds can always be found standing in water. The cautionary story, which uses flamingos as symbols of envy and vanity, is still very popular in Quiroga's native Uruguay.[23]

Tarot card readers have associated flamingos with even deeper and more spiritual meanings. The birds feature prominently in three decks: the Cosmic Tarot, designed by Norbert Losche; the Wonderland Tarot, produced by Morgana Abbey; and the Universal Fantasy deck, drawn by Paolo Martinello. In the first, the flamingo appears in the Star card, standing alongside a naked

Illustration from a modern reproduction of Horatio Quiroga's 'The Flamingos' Socks', 2010.

woman who is pouring water from two chalices into a wetland pool. The Star card is generally interpreted as looking towards a future that will bring something new and different. Some tarot readers have suggested that flamingos are included in this image because of their ability to undergo a metamorphosis – the colour change caused by variations in their diet.[24] In the Wonderland Tarot the suit of flamingos replaces the spades that would be found in a typical deck of playing cards. This suit associates them with the element air, and their appearance in a reading is related to conflict, sorrow and the mind – probably a fair association given how the poor birds were treated by the Queen of Hearts in Carroll's original tale.[25] The Ace of Chalices card from the Universal Fantasy deck shows a single large flamingo perched in the centre of a giant chalice overflowing with water. Chalices are associated with the element of water and, among other things, represent love. The association between flamingos and water is fairly obvious, but how the bird fits in to the rest of the card's symbolism is more mysterious. Perhaps it was deemed an appropriate symbol because of its romantic coloration, long lifespan and (perceived) long-term devotion to a single partner.

As these diverse examples show, the modern era of flamingos brought significant changes to how, where and why we see these birds. Although they previously made only occasional appearances in a few realms of human culture – mostly literature and paintings – they are now a hugely popular motif in nearly every realm imaginable. This transformation is merely the latest stage in the evolution of the millennias-old relationship between humans and flamingos; the birds may have started out as food in our stomachs but ultimately became firmly embedded in our collective consciousness. To fully understand exactly how that happened, it is necessary to consider one more flamingo landmark – one that occurred approximately halfway through the

The Star Card from the Cosmic tarot deck by Norbert Losche, 2006.

The Star

modern era, and forever changed how people think of flamingos. It was an event so culturally significant (to flamingos, anyway) that it deserves its own chapter. That event is the introduction in 1958 of the pink plastic flamingo.

4 A Breed Apart: Pink Plastic Flamingos

'Very tacky . . . garish, gaudy, tasteless, tawdry . . . carnival fare. Low class. Something someone would collect who knew nothing about art.'[1] These are the sentiments of artist Stella Rodriguez, a character in Susan Trott's novel *Flamingo Thief*, towards a flamingo figurine stolen by her husband. It is also an apt summary of public opinion towards another, vastly more popular, flamingo decoration – a 'pillar of cheesy campiness' that has been said to belong to 'the pantheon of American icons': the pink plastic lawn flamingo.[2]

This ornament, also known as *Phoenicopterus ruber plasticus*, is the brainchild of designer Don Featherstone, sculptor at and later president of Union Products, Inc. In 1957 Featherstone was asked to design a three-dimensional flamingo sculpture that the company could sell as a garden decoration. At the time, pink was a hugely popular colour, and could be found on everything from Cadillacs to household appliances to kitchen walls.[3] Also esteemed was the flamingo, a reminder of luxurious and 'pizzazzy' vacations to Florida and the Caribbean, where many Americans of the era had their first (and sometimes only) encounters with real, living versions of the bird. To Union Products, the time seemed right to add this cheerful species to the menagerie of decorative animals rolling off its assembly lines.

Portrait of a plastic flamingo.

Undeterred by an inability to procure a live model for his initial sketches, Featherstone based his work on flamingo photographs from a recent issue of *National Geographic* magazine. The original flamingo was sculpted from clay, around which a plaster cast was fitted; this was used to create moulds for the final plastic version of the product. The polymers used to fabricate the pink decorations are the same ones out of which acid shipping containers are created; they are, as a result, quite durable and can withstand environmental conditions in virtually any garden. Featherstone originally intended for the birds to stand on wooden legs, but because these would be too expensive to produce, the company decided to use metal instead.[4] The first batches of plastic flamingos were sold by Woolworth's, Ben Franklin and Sears, the last of which marketed the decorations as 'lifelike' and 'lovely' items that would improve the appearance of the owner's domestic landscape. The birds always came in pairs – one with its head and neck held erect, and the other bent over as though searching for food. Each pair was an affordable $2.76, which seemed a small price to pay to '[inscribe] one's lawn emphatically with Florida's cachet of leisure and extravagance'.[5]

Because plastic flamingos were originally most popular among families living in blue-collar neighbourhoods, and also because they were constructed of a cheap and common material, they were an object of derision in more artistic and upper-class circles. Soon enough, the presence of flamingos on the lawn had become a symbol of aesthetic illiteracy – a sign that the landscapers were cheap and tacky rather than chic and tasteful. The ornaments were so reviled that neighbourhoods and townships drafted laws against the installation of pink flamingos – and, when residents bent the rules by displaying flamingos of other hues, of any flamingo at all.[6]

Director John Waters's film *Pink Flamingos* (1972) only served to reinforce the idea that 'pink flamingo' is synonymous with 'tacky'. Waters called the movie in general 'an exercise in poor taste', and one of the film's many visual references to this theme is a pair of plastic flamingos placed in front of the mobile home belonging to Babs Johnson, the main character. Waters's use of this imagery is a nod to the popularity of these decorations in his hometown of Baltimore, Maryland. The film's final scene features one of the most notorious moments in cult cinematic history: the consumption of dog faeces by Babs Johnson, as played by drag queen Divine. This later inspired the comedian Randy 'Yappy' Fox to hold the annual Pink Flamingo Challenge, during which moviegoers attempt to eat food – usually chocolate – while watching the end of the movie. Those who find it too disgusting may benefit from 'Pink Phlegmingo' vomit bags often handed out during screenings of the show.[7]

During the 1960s gay men adopted the pink flamingo as an emblem advertising their sexual orientation; it has been suggested that the campness of *Pink Flamingos*, as well as the homosexuality of both Divine and John Waters, helped cement this symbolic use of the decorative birds. Even today plastic flamingos are used as batons in the Pink Flamingo Relay at the International Gay and Lesbian Aquatic Championships.[8] This tradition dates back to the 1990 'Gay Games III' in Vancouver and allows athletes a chance to let loose on the final day of competition by wearing costumes and indulging in silly behaviour. Flamingo symbolism has also been used by the gay-oriented Flamingo Auto Group South, a 'car club for men who prefer men in the driver's seat'.[9] Tomer Eshed, an Israeli film director, put a spin on the 'gay flamingo' theme in 2011 with his short film *Flamingo Pride*, which follows the exploits of the only straight flamingo in a flock of homosexual birds.[10]

Their prominence in the homosexual community notwithstanding, flamingos generally dropped out of favour during the 1960s and '70s; the Sears catalogue stopped selling the plastic birds in 1970. The declining popularity of the bright pink ornaments has been ascribed to two major factors: the hippie movement, which inspired people to use earthier, more organic-looking decorations, and the difficulties of the Vietnam War, which rendered Americans generally more sombre and less carefree. In this atmosphere, Union Products' gaudy pink plastic ornament was seen as decidedly kitschy and inappropriate. In the early 1970s the company briefly attempted to stem the tide of public opinion by marketing a 'flamingo deluxe', which came with more natural wooden legs rather than the metal rods featured on the original model. This did not help to improve the lawn birds' popularity, and they began to fade into obscurity.

Photographic proof that decorating with pink plastic flamingos can become addictive.

Historian Jennifer Price writes that when plastic flamingos did appear during this era, they were often being used by protesters looking to make some sort of social statement.[11] A classic example of this is the 'flocking' event that occurred on 4 September 1979 in front of the dean's office on Bascom Hill on the University of Wisconsin – Madison campus. The birds were installed by the Pail & Shovel Party, led by president James J. Mallon and vice president Leon D. Varjian, who formed their 'Absurdist Party' in time for the student body elections of 1978. Although they ran for office mostly as a joke – in order to protest a student government they found to be misguided and boring – they were re-elected the following year; the pink flamingo display was a sort of thank-you note to their faithful followers. The event is legendary to this day, and visitors to the campus can purchase postcards featuring photos of the original Bascom Hill flock. As far as anyone knows, only one of the original garden ornaments remains; Mallon and Varjian themselves donated it to the Wisconsin State Historical Society.[12]

It was not until the 1980s that the lawn decorations regained their place in the public's hearts and minds after appearing in the opening credits of the hugely successful television show *Miami Vice*. This association lent the birds a 'cool' factor they had not previously achieved. Instead of appearing in Sears catalogues, they were sold – at a more expensive $9.95 per pair – through outlets such as *Rolling Stone* magazine and Cat's Pyjama, a specialist store claiming to retail 'what you need to ruin your neighborhood'. By this point in time, baby boomers were fondly recalling the pink flamingos of their youths. This nostalgia persists today. Tom Herzing, who co-authored a book on plastic flamingos with Don Featherstone, says the birds remain popular because they '[remind] us that life can also be fun, that we should delight in the "small things"'. Further, he says, 'the pink plastic flamingo

. . . is a little fragment of our own character – the ability to be silly, a weariness with conventional notions of taste and beauty.'[13]

Whatever the psychological basis of Americans' love of *P. ruber plasticus*, it has resulted in the sale of over 20 million pairs of flamingos since 1957. The birds and their creator have also received nationwide recognition on a number of occasions. When the ornaments celebrated their thirtieth birthday in 1987, the governor of Massachusetts – their home state – declared them to be 'an essential contribution to American art'. In recognition of the need to help customers be confident they were buying genuine flamingo 'art' and not just a knockoff, Union Products took this opportunity to alter their moulds so that Don Featherstone's signature was featured just under the tail of every bird. A few years later, plastic flamingos were still a prominent enough symbol to be featured in the *Encyclopedia of Bad Taste* of 1990 and the *Whole Pop Catalog* of 1991. In 1996 Don Featherstone's artistic contributions earned him an Ig Nobel Art Prize, an award dispensed annually since 1991 by the scientific humour magazine *Annals of Improbable Research*.[14]

For the birds' fortieth anniversary in 1997, Featherstone visited the Universal Studios theme park in Orlando, Florida, which he decorated with a 500-bird flock of his iconic plastic ornaments. Although things appeared to be looking rosy for the birds, less than a decade later, in 2006, media outlets across the u.s. reported that Union Products would be closing – resulting in the immediate suspension of flamingo production. Public outcry was so extreme that another company soon bought the Featherstone moulds; these were subcontracted to and eventually purchased by Cado Products of Fitchburg, Massachusetts, the company currently responsible for the migration of plastic flamingos to lawns all over the u.s. and beyond. Fitchburg also happens to be the home of Don Featherstone, who, unsurprisingly, keeps a large flock of the pink birds in his garden – but only in summer, when they are weather-appropriate. During the winter, he prefers to decorate with 'Snomingos', an all-white version of his creation. Other variations of the flamingo theme are also available: the 'skel-a-mingo', a black-and-white Halloween-themed bird; the 'turkey mingo', for display at Thanksgiving; and the 'Christmasmingo set', comprising a 'Santa mingo' and four pairs of 'reinmingos'. Sports fans can even purchase flamingo pairs sporting the colours of their favourite teams' jerseys.

Some plastic flamingos have a purpose more noble than merely acting as decoration. Take, for example, the case of Floyd, a 'safety mascot' deployed each year by the North Central Region Avalanche Control Department working in the dangerous avalanche zone near the summit of Washington Pass. Floyd was first put into action by department supervisor Mike Stanford, who was looking for a way to remind his crews of just how dangerous their environment is; they had begun to ignore the 'normal' safety sign, and so Stanford gave them something a bit more obvious.

Floyd, the avalanche safety flamingo, standing 'knee'-deep in snow in Washington state.

Stanford says, 'It's the weirdest thing you would ever see in the mountains, in the snow. It's that hook to try and get people to pay attention and take notice.' He also points out that the flamingo is good for morale: 'Floyd adds a literal bright spot to the day for crews used to working in a world of white.'[15]

Another serious role of flamingos is as ambassadors of many fundraising campaigns across the country. Organizations engage in 'flocking', or making a surprise visit to a potential donor's house – often in the middle of the night – to distribute multiple pairs of the birds across the front lawn. The flock is often accompanied by a sign advertising the name and cause of the charity in need, and a 'reverse ransom' letter threatening to leave the gaudy display in place until the landowner provides a donation. It is not entirely clear how this fad began, but it may be related to the services provided by Flamingo Surprise, a Chicago company founded in 1991 when identical twin brothers Rick and Ralph Fazio 'borrowed' pink flamingos from several yards in Parma, Ohio, and then deposited them on their cousin's front lawn as a mischievous birthday present. When the brothers were approached by a passer-by who hired them to repeat the prank in honour of his wife's birthday, the pair realized they had stumbled upon an innovative way to help people celebrate special occasions.[16]

Flocking is a particularly popular technique among student organizations, such as teenagers looking to fund social gatherings or class trips. Unsurprisingly, many cancer charities have also adopted this practice because of the chromatic connection between flamingos and the pink ribbons typically used to generate awareness about breast cancer; 'Flock This Way', for example, is an annual fundraiser held in North Myrtle Beach, South Carolina, in association with the American Cancer Society.[17] In late 2011 the Lubben family of Geneva, Illinois, advertised their military-related charitable activities via a campaign they called 'Project Pink Flamingo'. Neighbours were asked to place a plastic flamingo amid their traditional holiday decorations, and the Lubbens kept track of the birds on a large sign, labelled 'Flamingos on the Loose', placed in their front yard. Next to the sign was a box into which visitors could place books that the Lubbens then donated to Soldiers' Angels, a non-profit organization that seeks to improve the lives of American soldiers stationed overseas.[18]

Flocking has also been used by Noah Brokmeier (otherwise known as the Diabetes Dude) to raise awareness about his disease – and, in particular, how it affects children. Impressively, Noah first began his outreach work shortly after his diagnosis at the tender age of six; he adopted the blue flamingo as an eye-catching symbol for his campaign. In addition to sending plastic versions across the country for flocking efforts, Noah has also distributed blue flamingo-shaped rubber bracelets and stuffed animals, and makes public appearances with Dancing Danie, a *Phoenicopterus* mascot who teaches the 'Flamingo Glide'. Those who join the Diabetes Dude in his campaign are known as members of The Flock.[19]

Although many people find flocking fun and entertaining, the practice has also garnered criticism. Some 'flockees' have accused their 'flockers' of trespassing and vandalism, as well as claiming that the term 'flocking' has a negative connotation because of its similarity to a certain swear word.[20] In one New York town, a flocking incident even made the police blotter after a resident called the authorities because she feared the birds had been placed with malicious intent.

P. r. plasticus flocks are also known to appear as art installations, such as those on display during the South Texas Botanical Gardens and Nature Center's 'Flamingo Fandango' and the

Flamingos On the Loose decorations in the front yard of the Lubben family, who use plastic flamingos to raise money for a military charity.

Quad Cities Botanical Center's 'Flamingo Fling'. Both events give artistically inclined locals an opportunity to provide 'naked' flamingos with elaborate and entertaining costumes; the birds are then distributed throughout the gardens so that visitors can enjoy both the flora and the plastic fauna. During the Flamingo Fandango, judges select one 'best of show' entry and then award prizes for categories such as 'All-American', 'Floral Creation' and 'Glitz, Glam and Sparkle'. The Flamingo Fling, on the other hand, culminates in a flamingo auction, allowing phoenicopteriphiles to bid on their favourite birds.[21]

Flamingo alteration also formed the basis of San Diego gardener Susi Torre-Bueno's 'Flamingo Parade', a collection of hand-painted birds distributed throughout her otherwise sophisticated garden. Torre-Bueno, a member of the San Diego Horticultural Society's Board of Directors, added these avian ornaments after being inspired to incorporate a few more 'whimsical objects' into her display. With the assistance of some friends, she painted

The Grand Flamale, an entry in the 'Flamingo Fandango'.

the flamingos with a range of costumes, from Egyptian queen to Oxacan carving to 'snowbird' (pensioners who go south for the winter). Torre-Bueno had no further plans for the display, but a friend entered a photograph of the garden into the online 'International Tacky Yard Art Contest'. The judges found the flamingos too well designed to be considered 'tacky', but appreciated the installation so much that they awarded its owner a blue gazing globe that is still in her garden to this day. When asked to guess why viewers found such delight in her flamingo art, Torre-Bueno points to their 'cocky attitudes [and] their refusal to be "merely" plastic birds'.[22]

As fun as these carefully curated flamingo exhibits may be, the infectiousness of 'phoenicopteriphilia' is perhaps best demonstrated by the number of informal flamingo displays erected by fans across the country and even around the world. In the u.s. a classic representation of summer vacation is a pair of flamingos plunged into the ground in front of a parked caravan; some camper owners even affix the flamingos to their grilles to act not only as a holiday mascot but also a masthead. Another popular practice is taking photographs of the plastic birds at iconic vacation destinations – the Statue of Liberty, for instance, or the Grand Canyon – as well as in unusual locations such as ski slopes.

The hobby is so widespread that Don Featherstone had no problem collecting hundreds of these photos to celebrate the birds' fortieth birthday; several of the images were later included in his book *The Original Pink Flamingos: Splendor on the Grass*. Although the obsession with plastic flamingo photography originated in the u.s., it has become an increasingly international affair. The website of Get Flocked, a plastic flamingo distributor, features an album of flamingo photographs snapped by American military personnel stationed overseas; the plastic birds are shown in places like Mosul, Baghdad and the Green Zone. The company first connected with soldiers after an American military paramedic ordered a pair of the birds to add a bit of colour to his military base in Iraq; the company responded by donating eight flamingos for free. Their very pleased customer mailed them a thank-you note saying that the birds had 'brought nothing but smiles to the people who see them', and that 'the flamingos are pure Americana and I'm sure they will be delighting dozens of people a long way from home for many weeks to come.'[23]

The Internet has also helped civilian flamingo enthusiasts connect via websites such as Flickr, where Fred Bayley began the group Pink Flamingo Fun to help phoenicopteriphiles share their images with each other and the world; the repository currently contains approximately 1,600 photos contributed by 160 members. Bayley's interest in the birds began when his staff responded enthusiastically to a flock he installed outside their office at work. They would dress the birds up at holidays and place them on display in order to bring smiles to the faces of passers-by – supporting Don Featherstone's opinion that plastic flamingo lovers are intrinsically friendly people. The success of this inadvertent bonding exercise inspired Bayley to keep an eye out for the plastic creatures in other locations. To this day, he holds up his flamingo experience as an example of how a single object can forge connections among disparate individuals.[24]

Bayley is not the only one to experience a sense of togetherness fostered by flamingos. Dale Duda, a resident of Northbrook, Illinois, and a member of the village's Community Relations Commission, introduced the practice of Flamingo Fridays, gatherings 'designed to bring people together in a world where jobs, kids' appointments, mobility, and other commitments and responsibilities make it difficult to get to know the people who live right next door'. Hosts advertise the upcoming events by placing a pink plastic flamingo on their lawns early in the week. Come Friday, residents arrive with their own chairs and refreshments, and the birds are passed from one week's host to the next. Duda reports that the events have transformed the community by giving neighbours a chance not only to socialize and have fun, but to share important news; following one Flamingo Friday, for example, residents coordinated to take care of an ailing neighbour after her condition was revealed during the social event. Several other American neighbourhoods have initiated similar flamingo-themed bonding opportunities.[25]

Flamingo Fridays in Northbrook, Illinois, are advertised with pink plastic garden flamingos put on display early in the week.

While some believe plastic flamingos are merely a humble ornament, others have also found a deeper meaning to the pink flamingo craze. The writer and conservationist Terry Tempest Williams referred to the decorations as 'our unnatural link to the natural world', while the philosopher and garden writer Allen Lacy said they are a reminder that our gardens are 'the products of human beings cooperating with the natural order to create utility and delight'. After contemplating these two viewpoints, Jennifer Price concludes that the birds are a way to mark boundaries – between humans and nature, art and kitsch, good taste and bad.[26] And what does the birds' creator think? 'I really like how my flamingo looks – it's very graceful', he says. 'An empty yard is like an empty coffee table – it cries out for something . . . I did something that people enjoyed, something that amused people. That's so much more satisfying than, say, designing something destructive like the atom bomb.'[27]

5 The Future of Flamingos

Traded by Phoenicians, eaten by Romans, captured and exported by European colonists, and sport-hunted in the Mediterranean: flamingos have a long history of unpleasant interactions with humans. Although the birds now benefit from regulations protecting many of their habitats and minimizing their capture or export, the future of flamingos is by no means certain.

Egg-poaching is still prevalent in South America, and low levels of flamingo consumption are consistently reported from across the birds' ranges.[1] The illegal slaughter of dozens of adult birds caused an uproar in India in early 2012 – especially since it occurred during the Global Bird Watchers' Conference in Gujarat.[2] The birds are also known to be negatively impacted by nearly all forms of human traffic, including planes, boats and all-terrain vehicles. The noise and visual disturbance caused by these vehicles disrupts feeding and breeding efforts and may even lead to habitat abandonment.[3] Ironically, much of this traffic is associated with ecotourism activities that are supposed to generate funds for protecting the birds over the long term.

Even more worrying is the degradation of flamingo habitats by human activities such as mining, farming and urban expansion. These can reduce the quality of feeding and breeding sites by altering water pH, introducing invasive species that out-compete flamingos for food, removing water (for use in irrigation or to facilitate easier access to minerals) and introducing dangerous structures such as power lines, with which flamingos can become entangled while flying.[4] In the Mediterranean, where native greater flamingos often come into contact with escaped lesser, Chilean and American flamingos, researchers worry about the potential detrimental genetic and behavioural effects of mixed-species breeding attempts.[5]

One of the most contentious issues is the proposed construction of roads through irreplaceable flamingo habitats. Perhaps the most well-known example of this looming threat is the on-again, off-again plan to build a highway in Tanzania to provide developers and industrialists access to the shores of Lake Natron – the single most important breeding ground in the world for lesser flamingos. As detrimental as the road itself could be, even worse is the accompanying plan to open a soda extraction plant that could alter water levels at the lake, thereby potentially reducing the quality and quantity of food available to the birds.[6] Adding their voices to the chorus of anti-development conservationists are locals whose livelihoods depend on the tourists who visit Lake Natron to see its masses of flamingos.[7] Road installation has also been proposed near the 'flamingo city' in the Rann of Kutch. The Gujarat State Public Works Department claims the highway is needed to meet the transportation needs of security forces and ecotourists. Biologists, however, fear that construction will alter water flow and reduce the accessibility of vital flamingo food resources.[8]

Although each of the six phoenicopter species is facing its own combination of existing and/or potential conservation issues, all of the birds may suffer equally from the effects of climate change. Flamingos are incredibly sensitive to the subtle variations in temperature and precipitation that dictate habitat suitability. Changing weather patterns could dry up favourite pools or flood them to the point that they no longer have the pH required to sustain the birds' primary prey; another worry is that changing water conditions might encourage blooms of toxic algal species or the spread of harmful bacteria.[9] Fluctuating water levels could also result in mud that is either too stiff or too watery for nest construction. As a result, flamingos may forego breeding. Although it is true that some phoenicopter populations have readily adapted to anthropogenic environments,[10] this seems to be the exception rather than the rule. Thus it would not be easy to provide flamingos with man-made alternatives to their preferred natural habitats; the widespread loss of feeding and breeding areas would likely lead to catastrophe.

Currently, the situation is most dire for the 'near-threatened' puna, Chilean and lesser flamingos; close on their heels is the 'vulnerable' Andean flamingo, while greater and American flamingos are, happily, considered to be of 'least concern' (though there is increasing worry over local extirpations of the latter species). Conservationists have already initiated several efforts to get the threatened birds out of harm's way. Important habitats for the South American species have been given official protected status, and activists are hard at work to achieve a similar goal at Lake Natron and other African lesser flamingo haunts. Anti-poaching laws have been introduced in some regions and guards have been hired to protect flamingo colonies throughout the breeding season.[11] Perhaps most importantly, researchers around the world have been working on surveying a growing number of flamingo habitats. These intensive efforts are vital for finding out exactly where the birds spend their time; without this information, environmentalists do not know which areas need to be protected. Censuses are important not only for providing accurate counts for each species, but for indicating whether populations are stable or fluctuating. Unfortunately,

A 'near-threatened' lesser flamingo takes advantage of favourable water conditions at Kenya's Crater Lake.

the distribution of species over vast areas of space, as well as the birds' tendency to roam from one place to another relatively frequently, make such geographic and demographic data very difficult to collect. Expeditions require large, coordinated groups of researchers and volunteers and, of course, quite a bit of time and money. Public awareness efforts such as BirdLife International's 'Think Pink' campaign and the Wildfowl & Wetlands Trust's Adopt a Flamingo programme are aimed at increasing the profile of flamingos in need, as well as generating funds that can be used for important preservation work.

Captive birds and aviculturists are just as important to flamingo conservation as wild birds and field researchers. Over the years, observations of captive birds have provided a wealth of information on flamingo physiology, morphology, behaviour and demographics. This is particularly true of the three South American species, which are difficult to locate and study in the wild.

Humans have successfully held flamingos in captivity for thousands of years.[12] One of the oldest private collections of captive flamingos can be found at the Copenhagen Zoo, which has housed various species of flamingo since 1881. Flamingos were not known to breed in captivity until 1937, when a pair of American flamingos produced an egg at the Hialeah Park racetrack in Florida; unfortunately, the hatchling died after two weeks of hand-rearing. However, just a few years later, in 1942, Hialeah Park was the site of the first documented successful captive breeding attempt.

A young flamingo fitted with a transmitter backpack so that its habitat use can be mapped.

Flamingo chick born at WWT Slimbridge, Gloucestershire – one of the world's premier flamingo-breeding facilities.

Researchers have offered several theories as to why flamingos have such difficulty breeding in anthropogenic settings. Pinioning, or snipping of flight feathers to prevent birds from flying away, may make it difficult for males to balance on females' backs during copulation. Small flock size may also be problematic. The birds will almost never breed in groups of fewer than ten individuals, and the 'magic number' for encouraging reproduction efforts appears to be 40 individuals; the one exception to this rule of thumb is the American flamingo, which seems willing to breed in relatively small numbers – such as on the Galapagos Islands, where the population size has always been rather low.[13] Some facilities have attempted to trick the birds into thinking they have more neighbours by installing mirrors throughout their flamingo enclosures; however, aviculturist Phil Tovey reports that this causes some narcissistic birds to become a bit self-obsessed and spend more time looking at their own reflections than wooing potential mates. Other persuasion tactics employed over the years have included using sprinklers to mimic the onset of the rainy season and installing artificial nests to spur potential breeders into action by making them believe their flock-mates have already begun nesting.[14] The latter technique has ultimately proven to be the most useful, and is routinely used by zoos, parks and private breeders around the world. Aviculturists at the Wildfowl & Wetlands Trust facility in Slimbridge further the ruse by inserting a fake wooden egg into one of the nests; after its appearance at the beginning of each breeding season, flock members are often observed touching it with their bills as if to check whether it is viable.[15]

The development of effective captive breeding protocols has been a long-term goal for two major reasons. First, if sustainable captive populations can be maintained in private collections, it will no longer be necessary to import wild-caught birds – a process that is always associated with the risk of injury and death to the birds during both trapping and shipping.[16] Second, maintenance of a large and healthy global population of captive birds

Fake flamingo eggs such as these from WWT Slimbridge can be used to prompt breeding attempts in captive birds.

Flamingo food pellets are soaked in water so captive flamingos can feed using their normal filtering technique.

acts as an insurance policy against any catastrophes that happen in the wild. Captive flamingos may some day be an important source of genetic diversity required for re-invigorating wild stocks, or, if captive breeding programmes reach their full potential, they could even be used to produce birds that can be released into natural flamingo habitats. Neither of these options is as attractive as developing conservation programmes that maintain and improve the health of current wild flocks, but they would be invaluable options as a back-up plan.

Keeping captive flamingos happy involves more than just optimizing breeding protocols, and it was years before aviculturists managed to master one of the most fundamental requirements of all animals: food. In fact, keepers are still hard at work perfecting food mixtures for each species in order to improve consistency and get the right mix of vitamins and minerals – and, of course, carotenoids. Early captive diets were often adequate for flamingo survival but failed to give the birds their characteristic hue; in addition to decreasing the enthusiasm of zoo spectators, this was also hypothesized to reduce the birds' interest in breeding with each other. Researchers did not really approach the problem from a scientific perspective until the 1950s, at which point they experimented with a number of different food components that they hoped would 'pink up' the birds; these included grass clippings, paprika, fish and shrimp, alfalfa and maize.[17] Modern pellets are made from a vitamin-supplemented mixture of wheat, fishmeal, soya and maize, with prawn meal and Carophyll® red thrown in to keep up the birds' colour. The pellets are sprayed with water until the mixture takes on a soupy consistency; captive birds are then able to use their natural filter-feeding technique to extract food particles.

Advances in these sorts of husbandry techniques are also invaluable to rehabilitators who may be required to care for injured wild flamingos. Flamingo researcher H. H. Berry described a 1975 effort aimed at rescuing and hand-raising 40 lesser flamingo chicks abandoned by their parents in the Etosha salt pan in Namibia; a good portion of the chicks eventually died, while those that survived were stunted.[18] Berry laments the lack of 'a more scientifically planned diet' that might have improved the birds' likelihood of fledging successfully. Thanks to the quality of contemporary commercial mixtures, hand-rearing efforts are now much more fruitful – though still unavoidably labour- and time-intensive.

Because health is mental as well as physical, aviculturists have also been trying to figure out how to keep their flamingos happy. Perhaps unsurprisingly, given the fact that where there is one flamingo, there is usually another, an integral part of

Slimbridge flamingos socializing in distinct groups – one, or even two, in the foreground, and another in the distance.

happiness is a satisfactory social life. Field researchers were responsible for first noticing that 'friendships' and 'coalitions' tend to form among pairs and groups of flamingos, and their work has since inspired in-depth research on flamingo relationships in captive flocks. These observations can help managers decide, among other things, what the optimal flock size is, how

much space birds need before they start getting on each other's nerves and which sex ratios are optimal for promoting breeding behaviour; by being aware of which birds prefer to flock together, aviculturists can also avoid separating 'friends' when moving birds between enclosures or giving animals away to other facilities. Results from these studies are also interesting because they can be compared with data collected from other species and, therefore, potentially illuminate broader patterns across all social animals (including humans). Always keen to lead the way in flamingo husbandry research, the Slimbridge facility is currently hosting an in-depth project on social dynamics in captive flamingos; preliminary results are posted on its 'Flamingo Diary' webpage.[19]

Flamingo exhibits are some of the most popular attractions at zoos and parks around the world. In fact, because of the

Paolo Rivera's
Vitruvian Flamingo,
2005.

remote and inhospitable nature of flamingo habitats, captive environments are the only place where many people will ever be able to experience flamingos – the non-plastic variety, that is – at all. As such, these facilities are a vital tool in the campaign to raise awareness about the plight of threatened flamingos in the wild. Education efforts are also aided by the production of documentaries such as *The Crimson Wing* and *In the Pink*, and the unusual amounts of attention these gawky yet glamorous birds receive in the media.

Like the mythical phoenix for which phoenicopters may have been an inspiration, flamingos have been reincarnated, time and again, in the human consciousness: as a delicious indulgence, a mascot to rally behind, an embodiment of poor taste, and, now, an emblem of awareness for many groups in need – including, sadly, some of the pink birds themselves. Thanks to their unusual and unique physical attributes, flamingos have always caught our attention and have never failed to impress. Although they may look delicate and slight, these deceptively hearty birds manage to survive in some of the harshest habitats on earth, and have been doing so for millions of years. We can only hope that efforts to protect these animals and their habitats will keep these living fossils around to brighten many more days over the generations to come.

Timeline of the Flamingo

c. 5000 BCE	*c.* 2000 BCE	414 BCE	EARLY 1ST CENTURY CE
First known image of a flamingo is created by Neolithic humans in Spain	Logographic reference to flamingos in the Tomb of Mehu, Saqqara, Egypt	Aristophanes includes a flamingo character in *The Birds*	Vitellius eats flamingo tongue

1754	1793	1838	1876
Mark Catesby draws flamingos in *The Natural History of Carolina, Florida, and the Bahama Islands*	Buffon writes about the 'red flamingo' in his *Histoire naturelle*	John James Audubon publishes his groundbreaking flamingo painting	Launch of HMS *Flamingo*

1941	1946	1958	1962
Ted Grouva writes jazz standard 'Flamingo', later performed by Herb Jeffries and Duke Ellington, among others	The Flamingo Hotel & Casino built in Las Vegas by Bugsy Siegel and Meyer Lansky	Don Featherstone's plastic flamingo goes on sale	The first flamingo stamps are unveiled by Russia and Mauritania simultaneously

1589	16TH CENTURY	1681	1697
J. Sparke describes New World flamingos (in Richard Hakluyt's *Principall Navigations, Voyages, and Discoveries of the English Nation*)	John White creates his flamingo drawing 	Nehemiah Grew writes about flamingo feeding	William Dampier instigates the belief that flamingos incubate eggs while seated in a strange position

1882	1891	1901	1918
'Flamingo' first used to refer to a plant species 	Sir John Tenniel depicts Alice using a flamingo mallet 	*Harper's Encyclopaedia of United States History* states that Creek Indians wore flamingo feathers on their heads	Horacio Quiroga writes 'The Flamingos' Socks', published in *Jungle Tales*

1972	1974	1990	2011
John Waters's *Pink Flamingos* is released	Alexander Calder's *Flamingo* unveiled in Chicago	Gay Games initiates the Pink Flamingo Relay 	*Gnomeo and Juliet* features Featherstone the flamingo

References

INTRODUCTION

1 Keith Bildstein et al., 'Flamingo Science: Current Status and Future Needs', *Waterbirds*, XXIII (2000), pp. 206–11; Peter Scott, 'Introduction', in *Flamingos*, ed. Janet Kear and Nicole Duplaix-Hall (Berkhamsted, 1975), p. 13.

2 P. Bearman et al., eds, *Encyclopaedia of Islam (Second Edition)*, at www.brill.com, accessed 4 July 2013.

3 Wilson B. Bishai, 'Coptic Lexical Influence on Egyptian Arabic', *Journal of Near Eastern Studies*, XXIII (1964), pp. 39–47.

4 George-Louis Leclerc, Comte de Buffon, *The Natural History of Birds* (Cambridge, 1793), vol. VIII, pp. 431–48; Étienne Gallet, *The Flamingos of the Camargue* (Oxford, 1950).

5 Etymological history obtained from the *Oxford English Dictionary*, from entries for 'flamingo', 'phoenicopter' and each of the words and roots in the Latin names of the six species. The *Oxford English Dictionary* can be accessed online via www.oed.com.

6 These data were downloaded from the Paleobiology Database using the search term 'Phoenicopteridae'. The database can be accessed online via http://paleodb.org; Alden H. Miller, 'The Fossil Flamingos of Australia', *The Condor*, LXV (1963), pp. 289–99.

7 Chris R. Torres et al., 'A Multi-locus Inference of the Evolutionary Diversification of Extant Flamingos (Phoenicopteridae)', *BMC Evolutionary Biology*, XIV/36 (2014), available at www.biomedcentral. com. As this book went to press, results of a new genomic study revealed even more detailed information about flamingo

phylogeny and suggested slightly amended divergence dates for the phoenicopters. For more information, see Erich D. Jarvis et al., 'Whole-genome Analyses Resolve Early Branches in the Tree of Life of Modern Birds', *Science*, XXXXLVI/6215 (12 December 2014), pp. 1320–31.

8 Mayr, p. 157; Gerald Grellet-Tinner et al., 'The First Occurrence in the Fossil Record of an Aquatic Avian Twig-nest with Phoenicopteriformes Eggs: Evolutionary Implications', *PLOS ONE*, VII (2012), p. e46972.

9 George Kirby Yeates, *Flamingo City* (London, 1950), p. 173.

10 Malcolm and Carol Ogilvie, *Flamingos* (Gloucester, 1986), pp. 19–22.

11 Ibid., pp. 26–7.

12 Charles Darwin, *A Naturalist's Voyage Round the World* (London, 1860), p. 69.

13 Ogilvie and Ogilvie, *Flamingos*, p. 54.

14 Ibid., pp. 59–60.

15 Ibid., p. 63.

16 Ibid., pp. 44–6; Torres et al., 'A Multi-locus Inference'.

17 Geoffrey E. Hill, *Bird Coloration* (Washington, DC, 2010), pp. 63–70.

18 Juan A. Amat et al., 'Greater Flamingos *Phoenicopterus roseus* Use Uropygial Secretions as Make-up', *Behavioral Ecology and Sociobiology*, LXV (2011), pp. 665–73.

19 Penelope M. Jenkin, 'The Filter-feeding and Food of Flamingoes (Phoenicopteri)', *Philosophical Transactions of the Royal Society of London, Series B, Biological Sciences*, CCXL/674 (1957), pp. 401–93.

20 Ibid., p. 414.

21 Casey M. Holliday et al., 'Cephalic Vascular Anatomy in Flamingos (*Phoenicopterus ruber*) based on Novel Vascular Injection and Computed Tomographic Imaging Analyses', *Anatomical Record*, CCLXXXVIII (2006), pp. 1031–41.

22 Stephen Jay Gould, *The Flamingo's Smile: Reflections in Natural History* (London, 1987), pp. 23–39; Nehemiah Grew, *Musæum Regalis Societatis; or, a Catalogue and Description of the Natural and Artificial Rarities Belonging to the Royal Society and Preserved at Gresham College* [1681], at https://play.google.com, accessed 4 July 2013.

23 Graham R. Martin et al., 'Visual Fields in Flamingos: Chick-feeding versus Filter-feeding', *Naturwissenschaften*, XCII (2005), pp. 351–4.

24 Manuel Rendón-Martos et al., 'Nocturnal Movements of Breeding Greater Flamingos in Southern Spain', *Waterbirds*, XXIII (2000), pp. 9–19.

25 Robert Ndetei and Victor S. Muhandiki, 'Mortalities of Lesser Flamingos in Kenyan Rift Valley Saline Lakes and the Implications for Sustainable Management of the Lakes', *Lakes and Reservoirs: Research and Management*, X (2005), pp. 51–8.

1 FLAMINGO BEHAVIOUR

1 Robert Porter Allen, *The Flamingos: Their Life History and Survival with Special Reference to the American or West Indian Flamingo (Phoenicopterus ruber)* (New York, 1956), pp. 1–19.

2 Georges-Louis Leclerc, Comte de Buffon, *The Natural History of Birds* (Cambridge, 1793), vol. VIII, pp. 431–48.

3 More information about Tour du Valat can be found online at http://en.tourduvalat.org.

4 Malcolm and Carol Ogilvie, *Flamingos* (Gloucester, 1986), p. 13.

5 Matthew J. Anderson and Sarah A. Williams, 'Why Do Flamingos Stand on One Leg?', *Zoo Biology*, XXIX (2010), pp. 365–74; Laura C. Bouchard and Matthew J. Anderson, 'Caribbean Flamingo Resting Behavior and the Influence of Weather Variables', *Journal of Ornithology*, CLII (2011), pp. 307–12.

6 Matthew J. Anderson, 'Lateral Neck-resting Preferences in the Lesser Flamingo (*Phoeniconaias minor*)', *Flamingo*, XVII (2009), pp. 37–9; Matthew J. Anderson et al., 'Individual Differences in the Preferred Neck-resting Position of Caribbean Flamingos (*Phoenicopterus ruber*)', *Laterality: Asymmetries of Body, Brain, and Cognition*, XIV (2009), pp. 66–78; Matthew J. Anderson et al., 'Preferred Neck-resting Position Predicts Aggression in Caribbean Flamingos (*Phoenicopterus ruber*)', *Laterality: Asymmetries of Body, Brain, and Cognition*, XV (2010), pp. 629–38.

7 Étienne Gallet, *The Flamingos of the Camargue* (Oxford, 1950), pp. 43–4.

8 Virginia Mascitti and Fernando Osvaldo Kravetz, 'Bill Morphology of South American Flamingos', *The Condor*, CIV (2002), pp. 73–83.

9 G. F. Zweers et al., 'Filter Feeding in Flamingos (*Phoenicopterus ruber*)', *Condor*, XCVII/2 (1995), pp. 297–324.

10 Manuel Rendón-Martos et al., 'Nocturnal Movements of Breeding Greater Flamingos in Southern Spain', *Waterbirds*, XXIII (2000), pp. 9–19.

11 Catherine E. King, 'Captive Flamingo Populations and Opportunities for Research in Zoos', *Waterbirds*, XXIII (2000), pp. 142–9; R. H. Britton et al., 'The Daily Cycle of Feeding Activity of the Greater Flamingo in Relation to the Dispersion of the Prey Artemia', *Wildfowl*, XXXVII (1986), pp. 151–5.

12 Felicity Arengo and Guy A. Baldassarre, 'Patch Choice and Foraging Behavior of Nonbreeding American Flamingos in Yucatán, Mexico', *The Condor*, CIV (2002), pp. 452–7; Guy A. Baldassarre and Felicity Arengo, 'A Review of the Ecology and Conservation of Caribbean flamingos in Yucatán, Mexico', *Waterbirds*, XXIII (2000), pp. 70–79; Virginia Mascitti and Mónica B. Castanera, 'Foraging Depth of Flamingos in Single-species and Mixed-species Flocks at Laguna de Pozuelos, Argentina', *Waterbirds*, XXIX (2006), pp. 328–34.

13 Reuven Yosef, 'Individual Distances among Greater Flamingos as Indicators of Tourism Pressure', *Waterbirds*, XXIII (2000), pp. 26–31.

14 Keith Bildstein et al., 'Feeding Behavior, Aggression, and the Conservation Biology of Flamingos: Integrating Studies of Captive and Free-ranging Birds', *American Zoologist*, XXXIII (1993), pp. 117–25.

15 Leslie Brown, *The Mystery of the Flamingos* (London, 1959), pp. 66–7.

16 Nicolas Mathevon, 'Individuality of Contact Calls in the Greater Flamingo *Phoenicopterus ruber* and the Problem of Background Noise in a Colony', *Ibis*, CXXXIX (1997), pp. 513–17.

17 Jeanette T. Boylan, 'Sonographic Analysis of the Vocalizations of Chilean and Caribbean Flamingos', *Waterbirds*, XXIII (2000), pp. 179–84.

18 Ibid., p. 180.

19 Abel Chapman, 'Rough Notes on Spanish Ornithology', *Ibis*, II (1884), pp. 66–99.

20 M. P. Kahl, 'Ritualised Displays', in *Flamingos*, ed. Janet Kear and Nicole Duplaix-Hall (Berkhamsted, 1975), pp. 142–9.

21 Frank Cézilly and Alan R. Johnson, 'Re-mating Between and Within Breeding Seasons in the Greater Flamingo *Phoenicopterus ruber roseus*', *Ibis*, CXXXVII (195), pp. 543–6.

22 Chapman, 'Rough Notes', p. 72.

23 Kahl, 'Ritualised Displays', p. 142.

24 George Kirby Yeates, *Flamingo City* (New York, 1950), p. 162.

25 William Conway, 'Overview and Future Directions: The Summing-up', *The International Journal of Waterbird Biology*, XXIII (2000), pp. 212–13.

26 E. F. Stevens, 'Flamingo Breeding: The Role of Group Displays', *Zoo Biology*, X (1991), pp. 53–63.

27 Brown, *The Mystery of the Flamingos*, p. 83.

28 H. H. Berry, 'South West Africa', in *Flamingos*, ed. Kear and Duplaix-Hall, p. 56.

29 'Five "Greyat" Flamingo Chicks Hatch at Edinburgh Zoo', The Royal Geological Society of Scotland, press release, www.rzss.org.uk/media-centre, 10 October 2014.

30 J. W. Clark, 'Letters, Announcements, etc.', *Ibis*, VI (1870), pp. 439–42.

31 Yeates, *Flamingo City*, pp. 180–81.

32 Ibid., p. 173.

33 Christophe Toureno et al., 'Adult Aggressiveness and Crèching Behavior in the Greater Flamingo, *Phoenicopterus ruber roseus*', *Colonial Waterbirds*, XVIII (1995), pp. 216–21.

34 Brown, *The Mystery of the Flamingos*, pp. 87–8.

35 Personal communication with Phil Tovey, aviculturist at Wildfowl & Wetlands Trust Slimbridge (UK), March 2012.

36 Sam Kelton, 'Greater, the 83-year-old Adelaide Zoo Flamingo, Dies', at www.adelaidenow.com.au, 31 January 2014.

37 Kibiwott Koros, 'Dead Flamingo was Ringed in 1962 – KWS', www.allafrica.com, accessed 4 July 2013; Floris Steenkamp, 'Dead

Birds Trigger Bio-toxin Scare', www.informante.web.na, accessed 17 October 2012.

38 Terry Stevenson and John Fanshawe, *Birds of East Africa: Kenya, Tanzania, Uganda, Rwanda, Burundi* (Princeton, NJ, 2002), plate 15.

2 FLAMINGOS IN THE EARLY HUMAN CONSCIOUSNESS

1 Personal communication with ancient American art historian Margaret Jackson at the University of New Mexico, May 2011.

2 Robert Porter Allen, *The Flamingos: Their Life History and Survival, with Special Reference to the American or West Indian Flamingo (Phoenicopterus ruber)* (New York, 1956), pp. 1–19; Virginia C. Holmgren, *Bird Walk through the Bible* (New York, 1972), pp. 63–5, 102.

3 T. G. Beddall, 'Gaudí and the Catalan Gothic', *Journal of the Society of Architectural Historians*, XXXIV (1975), pp. 48–59.

4 George Amos Dorsey, *The Mythology of the Wichita* [1904], http://archive.org, accessed 4 July 2013.

5 Personal communication with Dr Richard Drass, Oklahoma Archeological Survey, University of Oklahoma, March 2012, and Dr David S. Rood, Department of Linguistics, University of Colorado, April 2012.

6 J. Ph. Vogel, 'Errors in Sanskrit Dictionaries', *Bulletin of the School of Oriental and African Studies*, XX (1957), pp. 561–7.

7 Brenda Rosen, *The Mythical Creatures of the Bible* (New York, 2009), pp. 148–9.

8 Herodotus, *The History of Herodotus* [440 BCE], http://classics.mit.edu, accessed 28 October 2012.

9 Leslie Brown, *The Mystery of the Flamingos* (London, 1959), p. 32; Carlo Mari, and Nigel Collar, *Pink Africa* (London, 2000), p. 49.

10 Allen, *The Flamingos*, p. 2.

11 Peter Scott, 'Introduction', in *Flamingos*, ed. Janet Kear and Nicole Duplaix-Hall (Berkhamsted, 1975), pp. 14–15.

12 R. G. Gunn et al., 'What Bird is That? Identifying a Probable Painting of *Genyornis newtoni* in Western Arnhem Land', *Australian Archaeology*, LXXIII (2011), pp. 1–12.

13 Henri Breuil and Miles Crawford Burkitt, *Rock Paintings of Southern Andalusia: A Description of Neolithic and Copper Age Art Group* (London, 1929), pp. 21, 30.

14 R. Dale Guthrie, *The Nature of Paleolithic Art* (Chicago, IL, 2006).

15 Personal correspondence with James P. Allen. Further details can be found in Allen, *Middle Egyptian: An Introduction to the Language and Culture of Hieroglyphs*, 2nd edn (Cambridge, 2010).

16 Salima Ikram, *Choice Cuts: Meat Production in Ancient Egypt* (Leuven, 1995), p. 28.

17 André Dollinger, 'An Introduction to the History and Culture of Pharaonic Egypt', www.reshafim.org.il/ad/egypt, accessed 28 October 2012.

18 W. Geoffrey Arnott, *Birds in the Ancient World from A to Z* (New York, 2007), pp. 86, 98, 274.

19 James George Frazer, *Folklore in the Old Testament: Studies in Comparative Religion, Legend, and Law*, www.archive.org, accessed 4 July 2013.

20 Scott, 'Introduction', p. 14.

21 Aristophanes, *The Birds* [414 BCE], http://records.viu.ca, 28 October 2012.

22 Allen, *The Flamingos*, pp. 2–3.

23 Heliodorus (trans. Thomas Underdowne, revised and partly rewritten by F. A. Wright), *The Æthiopica* (London, 1587).

24 Jennifer Dines, *The Septuagint* (London, 2004).

25 Holmgren, *Bird Walk through the Bible*, p. 65.

26 George-Louis Leclerc, Comte de Buffon, *The Natural History of Birds* (Cambridge, 1793), vol. VIII, pp. 431–48.

27 Allen, *The Flamingos*, p. 3.

28 Ibid., p. 4.

29 Stephen Jay Gould, *The Flamingo's Smile: Reflections in Natural History* (New York, 1985), pp. 23–39; Suetonius Tranquillus, *The*

Lives of the Twelve Caesars [121 CE], at http://penelope.uchicago.edu, accessed 28 October 2012.

30 Aelius Lampridius (translated by David Magie), *The Life of Antoninus Heliogabalus*, www.mattin.org/recordings/heliogabalus. html, accessed 4 July 2013.

31 Gould, *The Flamingo's Smile*, p. 24.

32 Aulus Cornelius Celsus (trans. W. G. Spencer), *De Medicina*, at www.perseus.tufts.edu, accessed 28 October 2012.

33 Buffon, *The Natural History of Birds*, p. 445.

34 Helaine Silverman and David Browne, 'New Evidence for the Date of the Nazca lines', *Antiquity*, LIV (1991), pp. 208–20.

35 A. Sprunt, 'The Caribbean', in *Flamingos*, ed. Janet Kear and Nicole Duplaix-Hall (Berkhamsted, 1975), p. 66; Keith L. Bildstein et al., 'Feeding Behavior, Aggression, and the Conservation Biology of Flamingos: Integrating Studies of Captive and Free-ranging Birds', *American Zoologist*, XXXIII (1993), pp. 117–25.

36 Benson Lossing, ed., *Harper's Encyclopedia of United States History*, at www.perseus.tufts.edu, accessed 28 October 2012.

37 Pakistan Defence, 'Warfare in Ancient India', www.defence.pk, 15 November 2008.

38 P. Bearman et al., eds, *Encyclopaedia of Islam (Second Edition)*, at www.brill.com, accessed 4 July 2013.

39 Sayyid Saeed Akhtar Rizvi, 'The Scholarly Jihad of the Imams', *Al-Serat: A Journal of Islamic Studies*, www.al-islam.org, accessed 28 October 2012.

40 T. Morrison, 'Conservation in South America', in *Flamingos*, ed. Kear and Duplaix-Hall, p. 81.

41 F. J. Koning and J. Rooth, 'Greater Flamingos in Asia', in *Flamingos*, ed. Kear and Duplaix-Hall, p. 34.

3 THE RISE OF THE MODERN FLAMINGO

1 Etymological history obtained from the *Oxford English Dictionary*, from entries for 'flamingo', 'phoenicopter' and each of the words

and roots in the Latin names of the six species. The *Oxford English Dictionary* can be accessed online via www.oed.com.

2 Information obtained from www.jaquesamerica.com/croquet/how-it-all-began, accessed 4 July 2013.

3 Personal communication with representatives of Ubisoft, December 2011.

4 Malcolm and Carol Ogilvie, *Flamingos* (Gloucester, 1986), p. 65.

5 Leslie Brown, *The Mystery of the Flamingos* (London, 1959), p. 84.

6 Kay Ryan, 'Flamingo Watching', *Flamingo Watching*, www.poetryfoundation.org/poem/172270, accessed 4 July 2013.

7 Tony Manfred, 'Injured LeBron James gets Taunted by an Inflatable Flamingo', www.businessinsider.com, 25 May 2012.

8 Cynthia R. Fagen, 'Saved Flamingo Back in the Pink', *New York Post*, www.nypost.com, 7 November 2011; 'Wayward Flamingos Looking for Acceptance', www.caller.com, 11 April 2012; 'Escaped Flamingo Fiona pays Flying Visit to Reserves', www.bbc.co.uk, 12 May 2011; Stephen Pullinger, 'Tickled Pink by Exotic Strumpshaw visitor', www.edp24.co.uk, 11 May 2011; Jonathan Barnes, 'Aldeburgh: Fiona the Escaped Flamingo Spotted Back in Suffolk', www.eadt.co.uk, 4 February 2012.

9 Paul Rose, 'Flamingo Diary', www.wwt.org.uk/visit/slimbridge/diaries/flamingo-diary, accessed 4 July 2013.

10 Various authors, 'Flamingo', *Uncyclopedia*, at www.uncyclopedia.wikia.com, accessed 10 November 2012.

11 Personal correspondence with April Geiger, July 2012; her website can be accessed at www.stripedflamingo.com.

12 Kim Sloan and Joyce E. Chaplin, *A New World: England's First View of America* (London, 2006).

13 Eleazar Albin, *A natural history of English song-birds, and such of the foreign as are usually brought over and esteemed for their singing: to which are added, figures of the cock, hen and egg, of each species, exactly copied from nature* (Cambridge, 1737), at www.archive.org; John Latham, *A general synopsis of birds* (London, 1781), at

www.archive.org; Mark Catesby, *The natural history of Carolina, Florida and the Bahama Islands: containing the figures of birds, beasts, fishes, serpents, insects, and plants* (London, 1754), vol. I, at http://digital.library.wisc.edu; Alexander Wilson, *Wilson's American ornithology: with notes by Jardine; to which is added a synopsis of American birds, including those described by Bonaparte, Audubon, Nuttall, and Richardson* (Boston, 1840), at www.archive.org; Lear's artwork was published in John Gould's *Birds of Europe*, a five-volume series completed in 1837.

14 'American Flamingo, 1838', information from the National Endowment for the Humanities, http://picturingamerica.neh.gov, and 'Audubon's *Birds of America*', University of Pittsburgh, http://images.library.pitt.edu, accessed 4 July 2013.

15 Information provided by Kaitlin Beckett, May 2011. She can be contacted via www.a-curious-bestiary.com.

16 Information provided by Gesine Marwedel, March 2012. She can be contacted via www.gesine-marwedel.de.

17 'Flamingo Festival From January 7', *Deccan Chronicle*, at www.deccanchronicle.com, accessed 4 July 2013; '2010 Flamingo Festival', www.undp.kz, 11 September 2010.

18 Information from the Naval History Homepage (a collaboration between the National Museum of Royal Navy, Citizen Science Alliance Zooniverse and University of Oxford), at www.naval-history.net.

19 Royal Bahamas Defence Force, at www.rbdf.gov.bs, accessed 4 July 2013.

20 Guinness World Records, at www.guinnessworldrecords.com, 19 February 2011.

21 Personal correspondence with staff at the Ramstein Air Base, May 2011.

22 Bode Sowande, *Flamingo and Other Plays* (Harlow, 1986), pp. 1–52.

23 Horacio Quiroga, 'Las Medias de los Flamencos', *Cuentos de la Selva* (1918), at www.bibliotecasvirtuales.com (in Spanish), accessed 4 July 2013.

24 Information from user discussion fora on www.aeclectic.net.

25 Rachel Pollack, *Complete Illustrated Guide – Tarot: How to Unlock the Secrets of the Tarot* (New York, 1999).

4 A BREED APART: PINK PLASTIC FLAMINGOS

 1 Susan Trott, *The Flamingo Thief* (Raleigh, NC, 2010), p. 31.
 2 Don Featherstone and Tom Herzing, *The Original Pink Flamingos: Splendor on the Grass* (Atglen, PA, 1999), pp. 4–93; Jennifer Price, 'The Pink Plastic Flamingo', *American Scholar*, LXVIII (1999), pp. 73–88. This article is the source of the bulk of the historical information provided in this chapter.
 3 Joe Aaron, 'Flamingo Sounds Like a Nice Color', *Courier Press* (February 1958), http://m.courierpress.com.
 4 Monty Stanley, 'Why Not My Duck? An Interview with Don Featherstone: Pink Flamingos Turn Forty, part II', www.thegavel.net, accessed 10 November 2013; Steve Silverman, 'Pink Flamingos: So Tacky, Yet So Cool', www.uselessinformation.org, accessed 10 November 2012.
 5 Price, 'The Pink Plastic Flamingo', pp. 73–88.
 6 Joy Wallace Dickinson, 'Once Pink, Plastic Flamingos Come in Team Colors at Museum', *Orlando Sentinel*, http://articles.orlandosentinel.com, 20 October 2011.
 7 Michael Juliana, 'John Waters Talks Newspapers, Show Business, and *Pink Flamingos*', *Daily Trojan*, http://dailytrojan.com, 16 October 2012.
 8 'Pink Flamingo Relay', at www.acontrecourant.qc.ca, accessed 10 November 2012; Cyd Zeigler Jr., 'Top 10 Moments in LGBT Aquatics History', www.outsports.com, 20 October 2011.
 9 Johnny Diaz, 'Meet South Florida's Only Gay Car Club', *Sun-Sentinel*, http://sun-sentinel.com, 24 October 2011.
10 '*Flamingo Pride*: Berlin and Beyond Film', http://embassies.gov.il, 3 October 2012.
11 Price, 'The Pink Plastic Flamingo', pp. 73–88.
12 Wisconsin Historical Society, 'Bascom Hill Pink Flamingo', www.wisconsinhistory.org, 5 September 2005.

13 Featherstone and Herzing, *The Original Pink Flamingos*, p. 43.
14 More information available at www.ignobel.com.
15 Zoe Fraley, 'Plastic Flamingo Warns of Danger along North Cascades Highway', *Chicago Tribune*, www.chicagotribune.com, 5 May 2012.
16 More information available on the company's website, www.flamingosurprise.com.
17 Julie Roy, 'Barefoot Landing Gets Ready for Annual Flock Walk', www2.scnow.com, 27 December 2012.
18 Personal communication with the Lubben family, December 2011.
19 Personal communication with Tom Brokmeier, March 2012.
20 'Woman says Quincy HS Fundraiser is Vandalism', www1.whdh.com, 2 November 2011.
21 'Quad City Botanic Center Flamingo Fling call for entries', www.qconline.com, 11 April 2012; Personal communication with MaryJane Crull at the South Texas Botanical Garden, May 2012.
22 Personal communication with Susi Torre-Bueno, March 2012.
23 Personal communication with Betsy Krakowiak, www.getflocked.com, March 2012.
24 Personal communication with Fred Bayley (Flickr user Kiteline), May 2011.
25 Personal communication with Dale Duda, June 2011; Judy Peterson, 'Ready to Party? Look for a Pink Flamingo', www.mercurynews.com, 20 May 2011.
26 Price, 'The Pink Plastic Flamingo', pp. 73–88.
27 Stanley, 'Why Not My Duck?'

5 THE FUTURE OF FLAMINGOS

1 Alan R. Johnson, 'Flamingo Specialist Group: Past, Present, and Future Activities', *Waterbirds*, XXIII (2000), pp. 200–205; Sandra Caziani and Enrique Derlindati, 'Abundance and Habitat of High Andes Flamingos in Northwestern Argentina', *Waterbirds*, XXIII (2000), pp. 121–33; José A. González, 'Effects of Harvesting of Waterbirds and their Eggs by Native People in the Northeastern Peruvian Amazon', *Waterbirds*, XXIII (1999), pp. 217–24.

2 Himanshu Kaushik, 'Flamingo Poaching in Gujarat is the Worst-ever Across the Globe: Experts', *The Times of India*, http://articles.timesofindia.indiatimes.com, 20 January 2012. Ted Floyd, editor of the American Birding Association's *Birding* magazine and an interviewee in this article, informed C. R. Kight in July 2013 that, while the poaching discussed here *did* occur, his comments on the matter were fabricated by the author of this newspaper article; 'Flamingos Slaughtered for Meat in Kutch', *The Times in India*, http://articles.timesofindia.indiatimes.com, 4 January 2012; 'New Year Party Animals Feasted on Flamingo Meat', *The Times in India*, http://articles.timesofindia.indiatimes.com, 5 January 2012; Tanita Abraham and Nitya Kaushik, 'Flamingo Struggles for Life, Tells Tale of Pollution in Mudflats', www.expressindia.com, 18 May 2009; Japan K. Pathak, 'Photo Story of State-bird of Gujarat in Trouble', www.deshgujarat.com, 19 June 2011.

3 A. Luke, 'Spanish Pilots Force Flamingos to Flee', *New Scientist*, MDCCCXXXVII (1992), p. 7; Eduardo Galicia and Guy A. Baldassarre, 'Effects of Motorized Tourboats on the Behavior of Nonbreeding American Flamingos in Yucatán, Mexico', *Conservation Biology*, XI (1997), pp. 1159–65; Reuven Yosef, 'Individual Distances among Greater Flamingos as Indicators of Tourism Pressure', *Waterbirds*, XXIII (2000), pp. 26–31.

4 Durrell Wildlife Conservation Trust, 'Chilean Flamingo Species Factsheet', www.durrell.org, accessed 10 November 2012; Andrew R. Jenkins et al., 'Avian Collisions with Power Lines: A Global Review of Causes and Mitigation with a South African Perspective', *Bird Conservation International*, XX (2010), pp. 263–78; 'Killer Wires go Underground', *The Times of India*, www.timesofindia.com, 20 December 2011.

5 Frank Cézilly and Alan R. Johnson, 'Exotic Flamingos in the Western Mediterranean Region: A Case for Concern?', *Colonial Waterbirds*, XV (1992), pp. 261–3.

6 Wolfgang H. Thome, 'Tanzanian President's Motives for Serengeti Highway Becoming Clear', www.eturbonews.com, 2 April 2011.

7 Lawi Joel, 'Lake Natron Residents Prefer Flamingos to Soda Ash Plant', *DailyNews*, www.dailynews.co.tz, 12 September 2012.

8 'End of the Road for Flamingos?', *Deccan Herald*, www.deccanherald.com, 19 December 2011.

9 Robert Ndetei and Victor S. Muhandiki, 'Mortalities of Lesser Flamingos in Kenyan Rift Valley Saline Lakes and the Implications for Sustainable Management of the Lakes', *Lakes and Reservoirs: Research and Management*, x (2005), pp. 51–8; Charles Lugomela, Harish B. Pratap and Yunus D. Mgaya, 'Cyanobacteria Blooms: A Possible Cause of Mass Mortality of Lesser Flamingos in Lake Manyara and Lake Big Momela, Tanzania', *Harmful Algae*, v (2006), pp. 534–41.

10 Christophe Tourenq et al., 'Identifying Rice Fields at Risk from Damage by the Greater Flamingo', *Journal of Applied Ecology*, xxxviii (2001), pp. 170–79.

11 Species-specific information can be downloaded from the BirdLife International website, www.birdlife.org/datazone/species.

12 Robert Porter Allen, *The Flamingos: Their Life History and Survival, with special reference to the American or West Indian Flamingo (Phoenicopterus ruber)* (New York, 1956), pp. 1–19; Georges-Louis Leclerc, Comte de Buffon, *The Natural History of Birds* (Cambridge, 1793), vol. viii, pp. 431–48; Keith L. Bildstein et al., 'Feeding Behavior, Aggression, and the Conservation Biology of Flamingos: Integrating Studies of Captive and Free-ranging Birds', *American Zoologist*, xxxiii (1993), pp. 117–25.

13 Personal communication with Phil Tovey, aviculturist at wwt Slimbridge, March 2012; Simon P. C. Pickering and Laurent Duverge, 'The Influence of Visual Stimuli Provided by Mirrors on the Marching Displays of Lesser Flamingos, *Phoeniconais minor*', *Animal Behaviour*, xliii (1992), pp. 1048–50.

14 Elizabeth Franke Stevens, 'Flamingo Breeding: The Role of Group Displays', *Zoo Biology*, x (2005), pp. 53–63.

15 Personal communication with Paul Rose (biologist) and Phil Tovey (aviculturist) of wwt Slimbridge, March 2012.

16 A. Sprunt and A. Crego-Bourne, 'The Capture and Transport of

Young Caribbean flamingos', in *Flamingos*, ed. Janet Kear and Nicole Duplaix-Hall (Berkhamsted, 1975), pp. 103–5; J. E. Cooper, 'Capture in Kenya', in *Flamingos*, ed. Kear and Duplaix-Hall, pp. 106–8.

17 J. A. Griswold, 'Pigment Feeding', in *Flamingos*, ed. Kear and Duplaix-Hall, pp. 193–5; H. Wackernagel, 'Dietary Requirements', in *Flamingos*, ed. Kear and Duplaix-Hall, pp. 196–8.

18 H. H. Berry, 'South West Africa', in *Flamingos*, ed. Kear and Duplaix-Hall, pp. 53–60.

19 Information from Paul Rose, biologist and researcher at wwt Slimbridge; the Flamingo Diary webpage is www.wwt.org.uk/wetland-centres/slimbridge/diaries/flamingo-diary, accessed 20 November 2014.

Select Bibliography

Allen, Robert Porter, *The Flamingos: Their Life History and Survival,
with special reference to the American or West Indian flamingo
(Phoenicopterus ruber)* (New York, 1956)
AZA, EAZA and the WWT, *Flamingo Husbandry Guidelines*, published
online at www.flamingoresources.org/husbandry.html
Baldassarre, Guy A., Felicity Arengo and Keith L. Bildstein, eds,
'Conservation Biology of Flamingos', *Waterbirds*, 23 (special
publication 1) (2000)
BirdLife International, Global Species Programme data, published
online at www.birdlife.org/datazone/species
Brown, Leslie, *The Mystery of the Flamingos* (London, 1959)
Featherstone, Don, and Tom Herzing, *The Original Pink Flamingos:
Splendor on the Grass* (Atglen, PA, 1999)
Gallet, Étienne, *The Flamingos of the Camargue* (Oxford, 1950)
Gould, Stephen Jay, *The Flamingo's Smile: Reflections in Natural History*
(New York, 1987)
Jenkin, P. M., 'The Filter-feeding and Food of Flamingoes
(Phoenicopteri)', *Philosophical Transactions of the Royal Society of
London, Series B, Biological Sciences*, CCXL/674 (1957), pp. 401–93
Johnson, Alan R., and Frank Cézilly, *The Greater Flamingo*
(Berkhamsted, 2008)
Kear, Janet, and Nicole Duplaix-Hall, *Flamingos* (Berkhamsted, 1975)
Leclerc, Georges-Louis, Comte de Buffon, *The Natural History of Birds*
[1793], vol. VIII (Cambridge, 2010)
Mari, Carlo, and Nigel J. Collar, *Pink Africa* (London, 2000)

Ogilvie, Malcom, and Carol Ogilvie, *Flamingos* (Gloucester, 1986)

Price, Jennifer, 'The Plastic Pink Flamingo: A Natural History',
The American Scholar, LXVIII/2 (1999), pp. 73–88

Rose, Paul, 'Flamingo Diary', available online at
www.wwt.org.uk/wetland-centres/slimbridge/diaries/
flamingo-diary

Yeates, George Kirby, *Flamingo City* (London, 1950)

Zweers, G. F. et al., 'Filter Feeding in Flamingos (*Phoenicopterus
ruber*)', *The Condor*, XCVII/2 (1995), pp. 297–324

Associations and Websites

CAMPAIGNS

BIRDLIFE INTERNATIONAL'S 'THINK PINK' CAMPAIGN
www.birdlife.org/news/tag/think-pink

DURRELL WILDLIFE CONSERVATION TRUST FLAMINGO ADOPTION CAMPAIGN
www.durrell.org/adopt/chileanflamingo

WORLD WILDLIFE FUND (WWF) FLAMINGO ADOPTION CAMPAIGN
www.worldwildlife.org/gift-center/gifts/Species-Adoptions/Flamingo

WWT LESSER FLAMINGO ADOPTION CAMPAIGN
www.wwt.org.uk/flamingo

GENERAL INTEREST

AMERICAN MUSEUM OF NATURAL HISTORY – FLAMINGO RESEARCH
AND CONSERVATION
www.amnh.org/our-research/center-for-biodiversity-
conservation/research/species-based-research/birds/flamingos

FLAMINGO DIARIES AT SLIMBRIDGE WETLAND CENTRE
www.wwt.org.uk/wetland-centres/slimbridge/diaries/flamingo-diary

FLAMINGO SPECIALIST GROUP AT WETLANDS INTERNATIONAL

www.wetlands.org/Aboutus/Specialistgroups/FlamingoSpecialist Group/tabid/190

PINK FLAMINGO FUN FLICKR GROUP

www.flickr.com/groups/flamingo_fun

Acknowledgements

This book would not have been possible without the assistance of many generous, knowledgeable and patient people. Stephanie Kight and Paul Rose commented on early drafts of the manuscript; Christine E. Jackson gave valuable advice about how to research and write a book; staff at WWT Slimbridge (including Mark Simpson, Phil Tovey and Paul Rose) provided a tour of their facilities and arranged for me to use images from their flamingo photo archive; Linda DaVolls, Kim Downie, Iain Milne, Tony Longoria and Greg Kozatek helped me gain access to additional flamingo images hidden away in various libraries and databases; Martin Fowlie, of BirdLife International, provided flamingo literature and range maps; Rachel Browning (University of Exeter – Penryn Campus) and Rosie Sellwood (Falmouth University) provided tutoring in using research databases; James Allen, Felicity Arengo, Jeanette Boylan, Richard Drass, David Rood, Tim Brockmeier, Betsy Krakowiak, Mary Beth Henson, Dale Duda, April Geiger, Kaitlin Beckett, Kamala Dolphin-Kingsley, Susi Torre-Bueno, Fred Bayley, Gesine Marwedel, the USAF 435th Air Ground Operations Wing, MaryJane Crull, Beth Peters, the Lubbens and the Counselmans all patiently answered my flamingo-related questions; Victoria Gugenheim volunteered to paint a flamingo on my arm; and many photographers and artists donated their illustrations to the book free of charge. Thanks also to Brendan Godley, and the University of Exeter in general, for facilitating the trip to Kenya during which I saw flamingos for the first time. Thanks to the National Science Foundation for funding the fellowship during which I researched and wrote the majority of this book. Most importantly, thanks to my family and friends for giving me encouragement, putting up with my nonstop flamingo chatter, and filling my life with flamingo-themed trinkets over the past four years.

Photo Acknowledgements

The author and the publishers wish to express their thanks to the below sources of illustrative material and/or permission to reproduce it.

Adventureglass: p. 109 bottom left; Kaitlin Beckett: p. 100; Bloomsbury Publishing Plc: p. 75 (original drawing by Sir Peter Scott); Bridgeman Images: pp. 93 (Private Collection/Photo © Agnew's, London), 96 (Private Collection/Photo © Christie's Images), 107 (Private Collection/ DaTo Images); © The Trustees of the British Museum, London: pp. 74, 76, 94, 103 bottom; Daniela Cardone: p. 113; Caters: p. 89 (Tatiana Adamenko); Nick Cottrell/wwt Slimbridge: pp. 43, 139; © 1992 Disney: p. 106; Kamala Dolphin-Kingsley: p. 99; Debora Drower: p. 108 top right; Dale Duda: p. 131; Simon Ellison-Burns/wwt Slimbridge: p. 138; Elsevier: pp. 24, 25; Heidi Fischer: p. 120; Martin Fowlie/Birdlife International: pp. 31, 32, 33, 34, 35, 36; April A. Geiger: p. 91; Gerald Grellet-Tinner, Xabier Murelaga, Juan C. Larrasoaña, Luis F. Silveira, Maitane Olivares, Luis A. Ortega, Patrick W. Trimby and Ana Pascual: p. 12; Victoria Gugenheim (bodypainter and photographer): p. 102; Robert Hill: p. 26; Dave Irving: p. 66; C. R. Kight: pp. 21, 30, 46, 108 bottom left, 110 top and bottom, 136, 140; J. S. Lees/wwt Slimbridge: pp. 57, 61; Lubben family, Geneva, IL: p. 127; Graham Maples/wwt Slimbridge: pp. 16, 18, 19; Gesine Marwedel: p. 101; Bob McCreadie/ www.fabulousfred. co.uk: p. 92; Modernism Gallery: p. 105; Ryan G. E. Nelson: p. 81; Todd Oldham Studio: p. 97; Jeremy Paul: p. 98; U. Pieper, B. M. Webb, D. T. Barkan, D. Schneidman-Duhovny, A. Schlessinger, H. Braberg, Z. Yang, E. C. Meng, E. F. Pettersen, C. C. Huang, R. S.

Index